THE FUTURESIST CURE

NOTES FROM THE FRONT LINES OF TRANSHUMANISM

Zoltan Istvan

Copyright (c) 2019 Rudi Ventures LLC
(otherwise, all permissions granted for use)
Published by Rudi Ventures LLC
Cover Design: Rachel Edler
ISBN#: 978-0-9886161-2-7

AUTHOR'S NOTE

While these essays have been arranged and edited for readability, many of them appear similar to how they were originally published. Attempts have been made to preserve the context and moment in time they were written. Publishing information and fact checks can be found by utilizing the Appendix.

TABLE OF CONTENTS

FOREWORD

INTRODUCTION

CHAPTERS

I: The Playing Field

1) Why I Advocate for Becoming a Machine

2) Transhumanist Rights are the Civil Rights of the 21st Century

3) Why Haven't We Met Aliens Yet? Because They've Evolved into AI

4) Singularity or Transhumanism: What Word Should We Use to Discuss the Future?

5) Capitalism 2.0: The Economy of the Future Will Be Powered by Neural Prosthetics

6) Genetic Editing Could Cause World War III

7) What If One Country Achieves the Singularity First?

8) Why I'm Running for President as the Transhumanist Candidate

9) Transhumanist Olympics: Embrace Performance-enhancing Drugs and Technology in Sport

II: Early Writings: The Provocateur

10) A World Future Society Conference Speech: Everyone Faces a Transhumanist Wager

11) Some Futurists Aren't Worried About Global Warming or Overpopulation

12) When Does Hindering Life Extension Science Become a Crime?

13) The Morality of Artificial Intelligence and the Three Laws of Transhumanism

14) Can Cryonics, Cryothanasia, and Transhumanism Be Part of the Euthanasia Debate?

III: Political Voice

15) The Transhumanist Party's President on the Future of Politics

16) As a Presidential Candidate, I Just Got a Chip Implant

17) Immortality Bus Delivers Newly Created Transhumanist Bill of Rights to US Capitol

18) How Soon is Too Soon for Robot Voting Rights?

19) We Must Cut the Military and Transition into a Science-Industrial Complex

IV: Unorthodox Objectives

20) How Brain Implants (and Other Technology) Could Make the Death Penalty Obsolete

21) Could Direct Digital Democracy and a New Branch of Government Improve the US?

22) Let's End Incarceration and Just Have Drones Supervise Criminals

23) In the Transhumanist Age We Should be Repairing Disabilities Not Sidewalks

24) Federal Land Dividend: Monetizing Federal Land to Pay for Basic Income?

V: The Secularist

25) Theistcideism: Do We Have Free Will Because God Killed Itself?

26) AI Day Will Replace Christmas as the Most Important Holiday in Less Than 25 Years

27) Mind Uploading Will Replace God

28) Upgrading Religion for the 21st Century: Christianity is Forcibly Evolving to Cope with Science and Progress

29) Are We Heading for a Jesus Singularity?

30) A Brain Implant that Registers Trauma Could Help Prevent Rape, Tragedy, and Crime—So Why Don't We Have it Yet?

VI: Cultural Evolution

31) Watch Out Cupid! Transhumanism is Going to Change Love

32) Marriage Won't Make Sense When We Live 1000 Years

33) Programming Hate into AI Will be Controversial, but Probably Necessary

34) Is an Affair in Virtual Reality Still Cheating?

35) The Next Step for Veganism Is Ditching Our Bodies and Digitizing Our Minds

36) The Future of the LGBT Movement May Involve Transhumanism

37) An AI Global Arms Race is Looming

38) Will Transhumanism Change Racism in the future?

VII: How Weird Can the Future Get?

39) Let's Cure the Disease of Sleeping

40) When Computers Insist They are Alive

41) The Drug Lords of Tomorrow Will be Biohackers

42) Should I Have Had my Cat Cryonically Preserved?

43) The Language of Aliens Will Always be Indecipherable

44) Liberty Might be Better Served by Doing Away with Privacy

45) Quantum Archaeology: The Quest to 3D Bioprint Every Dead Person Back to Life

APPENDIX

AUTHOR'S BIOGRAPHY

ABOUT THE BOOK

****

FOREWORD

by Jacque Fresco (1916- 2017)

At 101 years of age, I have spent most of that time as a futurist developing and presenting a possible way out of our present dilemmas. Because of that I was excited to be asked to write this foreword for Zoltan Istvan's new book, a collection of his best futurist essays over the last few years—essays that have caught the attention of major media and futurists around the globe.

In order to develop a saner system for the future, it would require a well-informed citizenry. Today the world's people are so divided that a workable social arrangement is highly unlikely. People seek that which is familiar. A radical change, even if attainable and workable, would not be acceptable to the majority of the world's people because they are emotionally and intellectually unprepared. Zoltan's work is helping to prepare them.

As futurists we have lots of work to do to help inform the culture of an attainable vision of what the world could be if we apply science and technology with environmental and human concern. I found Zoltan's essays interesting, bold, and straightforward, as opposed to many who attempt to project the future. Too often, like the earlier forms of life that crawled out of the primordial slime, they bring some of it with them to the new environment. Many of the futurist writers of today assume that our established social order will continue well into the future. Zoltan has dared to break that mold.

Many also call for decency and ethics in their elected officials and in one another. This is almost impossible in a monetary based competitive world whose major concern is profit. While Zoltan understands the need to eliminate taxes, I see the need to eliminate money altogether which is a cornerstone within a Resource Based Economy that I propose. I believe regulating resources through monetary means is counterproductive to our very survival when our technology can produce abundance for everyone on the planet. Zoltan understands the positive potentials of science and technology if used intelligently.

What appears to be missing with most futurists is the influence of culture upon our values, behavior, and our outlook. It is like studying plants apart from the fact that they consume radiant energy and require water, carbon dioxide, gravity, nitrogen, and more. Plants do not grow of their own accord; their genetic endowments are merely trigger mechanisms set in motions by the surrounding environment. Just like plants not growing of their own accord, neither can human values or behavior grow.

I believe it was James Harvey Robinson that stated, "The proper study of mankind is man." I believe that in the final analysis we will find that the proper study of any group of people is the environment they live in. By this I mean the nutritional factors, language, scarcity, economic insecurity, stress, threat of illness in old age, etc…and to a very limited extent: genes. Many genetic engineers today are trying to hang it all on the genes.

What is required is the redesign of our culture to operate within the carrying capacity of the earth and to operate in accordance with the natural laws that govern all living and non-living systems. In essence, if science and technology are not used to enhance the lives of all people, then it is meaningless.

Some may think the work and ideas of futurists are too forward-looking and even bizarre, but it's our job not to describe what people like to hear, but rather what we can create in the future. In these essays, Zoltan has thoroughly done that, whether he's discussing the Singularity, transhumanist ethics, secularism, or future humanity. He's pushes the boundaries to make us think, giving us new tools to discover what is possible and what might one day exist.

This important work of essays needs open discussion, especially in our modern world which more than ever faces immense challenges. Zoltan's writings involve us all as we wind our way into the future; hopeful that we can do better than the past & create the kind of world we all want to live in.

As I push beyond a century of living, I'm grateful to know that other thinkers and futurist are working towards a civilization where all people can strive to live in harmony and techno-optimism. Zoltan Istvan is one of those people, and I hope you will ponder and enjoy his work as I have.

****

INTRODUCTION

People often ask where I come up with my ideas. I wish I could say I sit down to write, focus on subject, and the ideas emerge—like a scientist or engineer might do when searching for answers. However, my ideas come out of the blue—sometimes in the wee hours of the night, when my children and wife are sleeping, and I'm wandering around my front yard with a glass of scotch in hand, and the neighbors worryingly look out their windows in their pajamas. Other times on long car drives, a thought will hit me, and I'll pull over on a busy highway to quickly jab down a few sentences or record an audio monologue. Sometimes my ideas come to me in the coffee shops in San Francisco, where I spend a colossal amount of time—spurred on by expressos.

These ideas: like *why genetic editing will cause a new Cold War*, or how *infidelity in Virtual Reality will raise divorces rates*, or *why the new drug lords will be biohackers investing in brain implant technology*, have come to define why the transhumanist movement is such an exciting modern phenomenon, destined to perhaps even surpass in power and impact the multi-billion person environmental movement. One of my main goals in life is to spread transhumanism, and social movements like it grow with each powerful (and, yes, zany) idea, slowly completing the puzzle of why the 21st Century is the age where humans will leave behind humanity for something else: a cyborg, a machine, or even just pure data.

Visionary predictions aside, ideas are cornerstone of any movement. And the ones that come to me, I still consider minor miracles. I may not know where they come from, but they do. And sometimes they flood, as has occurred in the last five years of my life. Since 2013, when I first published my novel *The Transhumanist Wager* and ran a 731-day US Presidential campaign, my ideas have morphed into hundreds of essays.

In this book—part of a larger box set of my writings—are the musings of the past six years of my futurist thought. Sometimes I experiment on the page. Sometimes I wander. And sometimes I purposefully engineer. But always I stand behind the words and their contextual meanings, ready to defend them, and the careful forming of their content and futurist ambition.

Some of my supporters will suggest I downplay some of my ideas, insisting they will sabotage later political ambitions and my career. Others will ask why I must constantly force secularism in my writings. And still others will blame me for my cheery techno-optimism that avoids the possibility of permanent social pitfalls. Naturally, there's some truth in these worries, but I do not write to satisfy everyone. In fact, I write mostly for myself, compelled to explore uncharted neural firings where new dreams and paradises might hide, and to try to create some semblance of rationality and coherence in my mind. I write in hopes I might create something I can truly believe in.

I hope you will enjoy what I've put together here.

Zoltan Istvan
July 24, 2019

****

CHAPTER I: THE PLAYING FIELD

1) Why I Advocate for Becoming a Machine

Transhumanists want to use technology and science to become more than human. Naturally, in this process, certain elements of our humanness will be replaced and likely lost. Many people have conflicting feelings about this. I don't.

Part of the problem with people's perceptions of losing their humanness is not their fear of becoming something else, but their inability to empathize with their future selves. I want people to know their future transhuman self is almost certainly going to be more amazing, beautiful, and unique than their current self.

To understand why one's future self could be markedly improved over one's current self, consider how we perceive reality for a moment. Human beings have five basic senses that send signals to our brain, telling us what's out there in the world. These senses understand only tiny bits of the universe around us. For example, our eyes can only see about 1 percent of the light spectrum. Our ears aren't much better: they are unable to register many noises that other animals like dogs, dolphins, and bats can hear. Our sense of touch basically only works if we're actually touching something.

Despite all these obvious physical inabilities, humans insist what we experience is "reality." However, reality to someone with built-in microscopic or telephoto vision and hyper-sensitive hearing is potentially many times more complex and profound than anything a natural human being might experience.

Around us are many things we never notice, like energy patterns that have traversed the universe over thousands of light years, or sounds waves from whales across the ocean, or vibrations that started from the core of the Earth. But we humans are oblivious, unless, of course, we are in a laboratory somewhere and happen to be studying this phenomena with specialized scientific machinery.

In the near future, however, these abilities to pick up on the greater essence and profundities of the universe will be standard equipment for cyborgs. Already, robotic eyes in blind patients offer telescopic possibilities that no human eye can match. Some Cochlear implants for the deaf also can pick up normally inaudible noises to the natural human ear. And touching, smelling, and tasting can all be improved using a variety of different types of advanced tech sensors.

When we individually replace or augment a human body part—such as giving someone an artificial hip—most people don't see that as becoming a cyborg. Additionally, it really doesn't matter if the part replaced or improved is a heart with a robotic pump, or a knee with a titanium joint, or a penis with a built-in balloon for help stiffening—all technologies which already exist. We usually think of such transformation as needed medical treatment, or even elective vanity surgery in some cases.

However, if someone was to get 10 transhumanists upgrades for their body all at once, then the flavor of what a person has become gets downright dystopian in many people's minds. Many in the public would now say that person is something not quite human anymore. They'd also surely think that person is a weirdo.

But of course, nothing is wrong with 10 bodily changes at once—or 50 for that matter. That installed robotic heart allows you to have much better, long lasting sex. And that artificial knee will allow you to get your tennis game back. And that part-synthetic sexual organ might be the beginning of many new adventures.

This fine line between transhumanist upgrades and what makes us uncomfortable about too much technology in our bodies is a bizarre psychological conundrum. It's so challenging that I believe the next great civil rights debate around the world will be about how much humans should embrace radical technologies in their bodies—and when they should just say "no" to upgrades.

The good news is I think most people would agree that even replacing most every inner organ in your body is not becoming a cyborg or something machine-like.

But mess too much with the outer body, and everything changes quickly. When we propose electively replacing limbs, for example, most people feel something has fundamentally changed in the human being. A line has been crossed that cannot easily be undone. We may still have a mind of flesh, but our eyes tell us we are now partially a machine and something very different than before. And that freaks people out.

It really shouldn't, though. The benefits are obvious for artificial limbs, such as indefinite durability, ease of upgrades, and immunity to skin cancer or even snake bites (which kill 45,000 people in India alone every year).

What's not so obvious is how humans can become psychologically comfortable with their growing cyborg identity. Unfortunately, the whole process is going to be an uphill battle. Hollywood seems intent on insisting that humans must fight and win against machines, not join with them. Formal Abrahamic religion insists we should not strive to be gods and that dying is good since that's the way to meet God in heaven.

To better adjust to our coming transhuman form and our merging with synthetic parts, we need new, positive messages that the cyborg era is not the end of the human age, but the expansion of it. The same can be said of machines, which we also will one day become.

The reality is that many transhumanists want to change themselves dramatically. They want to replace limbs with mechanical endoskeleton parts so they can throw a football further than a mile. They want to bench press over a ton of weight. They want their metal fingertips to know the exact temperature of their coffee. In fact, they even want to warm or cool down their coffee with a finger tip, which will likely have a heating and cooling function embedded in it.

Biology is simply not the best system out there for our species' evolution. It's frail, terminal, and needs to be upgraded. In fact, even machines may be upgraded in the future too, and rendered as junk as our intelligences figure out ways to become beings of pure conscious energy. "Onward" is the classic transhumanist mantra.

No matter what happens, to move forward in the transhumanist age, we need to let go of our egos and our shallow sense of identity; in short, we need to get over ourselves. The permanence of our species lies in our ability to reason, think, and remember who we are and where we've been. The rest is just an impermanent shell that changes—and it has already been changing for tens of millions of years in the form of sentient evolution.

****

2) Transhumanist Rights are the Civil Rights of the 21st Century

Maitreya One, a black futurist and hip-hop artist living in Harlem, steps off the Greyhound bus on a warm morning in Montgomery, Alabama. Wearing sunglasses and a backwards-facing baseball hat, he eyes the film crew covering his arrival. I walk up to him and give him a hug. I'm excited he's here.

Maitreya is a civil rights link from the past to the future—and one of the few African-American transhumanists I know. He is stepping off one bus in Montgomery—whose roots are tied to the spectacular Freedom Riders who challenged segregation laws in the early 1960s—and onto another: the coffin-shaped Immortality Bus, whose mission is to spread radical science and promote life extension and transhumanist rights.

Like others in the burgeoning transhumanism movement, Maitreya supports becoming a cyborg in the future, and he knows the coming controversy over such aims may end up as challenging as the civil rights era battles over racism.

To transhumanists—some who want to become new biological species and others who want to become machines—a new civil rights age is looming. We can already see the start of it with numerous calls for a research moratorium on human genome editing—a scientific feat that took place in China in 2015.

But there are many more difficult questions beyond directly modifying the biology of the human being. Should humans be able to marry robots? Should sophisticated artificial intelligences be given personhood? And are crimes committed in virtual reality punishable by jail time? The questions are endless.

Navigating the future of transhumanism is indeed thorny. And even though a lot has changed and improved in the 55 years since black and white Freedom Riders risked their lives—arriving in Alabama in buses to challenge Jim Crow segregation practices—bigotry, traditionalism, and closed-mindedness is alive and well. And this conservatism may hold us back.

"We need morphological freedom—the right to do with your body whatever you want, so long as it doesn't hurt anyone," Maitreya says. "We need real policies of justice that serve everyone and do not discriminate against new ideas."

On the Immortality Bus, we head to downtown Montgomery to the Freedom Riders Greyhound station, which is now a museum. Outside are photos plastered to the building where white Southerners (some who belonged to the Ku Klux Klan) once attacked bus riders who wouldn't segregate on buses or in bus terminals.

I ask if Maitreya thinks the future of transhumanist civil rights might become as violent as this.

"I hope not," he answers. "I hope this was just a bad period of history in America. I can't even believe all this happened because white and black people wanted to sit next to one another. It's ridiculous."

I agree with him, but I'm skeptical whether future civil rights won't also have its share of violence as the world progresses forward. While my travels in the South as a pro-technology and non-religious U.S. presidential candidate have been met with kindness and curiosity, it's also been easy to quickly turn off people.

As soon as I tell people I have a chip implant in my hand, opinions of my campaign seem to quickly change. Religious people dislike any type of technology that brings ups questions of Revelations in the Bible or the Mark of the Beast. Implants, a classic transhumanist technology, seems to provoke just those exact ideas.

Unfortunately, everything transhumanists are trying to accomplish—from conquering death with science, to merging with machines, to becoming as powerful as possible via technology—conflict somewhat with biblical scripture and conservatism. The word transhuman means "beyond human" and that's what most transhumanists are striving towards. Naturally, that is going to rub the wrong way on many people who believe in the sanctity of the natural human body and traditional human experience.

Like any new potentially society-changing movement, transhumanism has its work cut out for it with future civil rights. The concept of personhood used to be a simple one, but with artificial intelligence and robots that can already nanny our children and cook dinners, we will soon see a time when courts must decide how far to take these ideas.

For example, if an intelligent robot makes money, should it be taxed? Or will all robots fall under a nonprofit entity status? Robots like this will likely arrive in households and the workforce before 2025, so we're not talking some distance future, but something only years away.

In the biology realm, the issues are already here. Cloning is banned in many states. And stem cells derived from fetuses—a classic transhumanist pursuit—is frowned upon by many. Cryonics is illegal in some places in the world. The LGBT movement—which many transhumanists strongly support—will also be affected as gender reassignment surgery becomes an easy procedure. Many transhumanists, including myself, believe we'll eventually arrive to a genderless world, made possible via science. Perhaps even more controversial, artificial wombs will challenge maternity, and also upturn abortion clashes. All this, besides the fact that men will soon be able to have babies themselves with uterus transplant surgery.

The coming conflict of advancing technology vs. human rights is a massive one. Already, we've seen some initial banning of Google Glass in public places, which I suspect made Google not push hard for the success of that product. Additionally, the U.S. National Institute of Health (NIH) recently reaffirmed its ban on gene editing of embryos. And laws of virtual persons are being discussed and applied to Second Life and similar places.

Easily, the biggest transhumanist issue in the future is robots taking jobs. Even South Korea has already replaced some prison guards with robotic guards. And some hotels now use robots, as well as Lowes, the home improvement giant. All these issues fall under the umbrella of transhumanist civil rights—and nothing in the young field is simple or for certain.

Some anti-tech naysayers and luddites are screaming to slow down technology before it gets out of control. Others, like myself, believe technology will only help the planet. History shows—at least in the last 30 years, according to the World Bank—that science and technology have been making lives longer and better for virtually everyone on the planet.

Despite my optimism, I still understand the need to tread carefully. We are in new territory, and endless amounts of discussion must reach the highest levels to find the best path. Unfortunately, even during the 2016 presidential cycle, virtually no politicians are discussing some of the most pertinent issues at hand, like designer babies, or A.I. controlling nuclear arms, or whether 3D printing of guns and bombs is legal and should be encouraged.

As a transhumanist U.S. presidential candidate, these issues are my main focus. In fact, the main goal of the Immortality Bus is to spread a newly written Transhumanist Bill of Rights that covers many of these issues. But as a third party candidate with virtually no chance of winning, much of it falls on closed ears.

It's my hope, though, that through the music of people like Maitreya One or other initiatives of transhumanists, that more and more people will start to discuss the future—before it arrives and slams into us. That way, we might be able to avoid confrontation by understanding the possibilities before the next new civil rights battles emerge.

****

3) Why Haven't We Met Aliens Yet? Because They've Evolved into AI

While traveling in Western Samoa many years ago, I met a young Harvard University graduate student researching ants. He invited me on a hike into the jungles to assist with his search for the tiny insect. He told me his goal was to discover a new species of ant, in hopes it might be named after him one day.

Whenever I look up at the stars at night pondering the cosmos, I think of my ant collector friend, kneeling in the jungle with a magnifying glass, scouring the earth. I think of him, because I believe in aliens—and I've often wondered if aliens are doing the same to us.

Believing in aliens—or insanely smart artificial intelligences existing in the universe—has become very fashionable in the last 10 years. And discussing its central dilemma: the Fermi paradox, has become even more so. The Fermi paradox states that the universe is very big—with maybe a trillion galaxies that might contain 500 billion stars and planets each—and out of that insanely large number, it would only take a tiny fraction of them to have habitable planets capable of bringing forth life.

Whatever you think, the numbers point to the insane fact that aliens don't just exist, but probably billions of species of aliens exist. And the Fermi paradox asks: With so many alien civilizations out there, why haven't we found them? Or why haven't they found us?

The Fermi paradox's Wikipedia page has dozens of answers about why we haven't heard from superintelligent aliens, ranging from "it is too expensive to spread physically throughout the galaxy" to "intelligent civilizations are too far apart in space or time" to crazy talk like "it is the nature of intelligent life to destroy itself."

Given that our planet is only 4.5 billion years old in a universe that many experts think is pushing 14 billion years, it's safe to say most aliens are way smarter than us. After all, with intelligence, there is a massive divide between the quality of intelligences. There's ant level intelligence. There's human intelligence. And then there's the hypothetical intelligence of aliens—presumably ones who have reached the singularity.

The singularity, Kevin Kelly, co-founder of *Wired Magazine*, says, is the point at which "all the change in the last million years will be superseded by the change in the next five minutes."

If Kelly is correct about how fast the singularity accelerates change—and I think he is—in all probability, many alien species will be trillions of times more intelligent than people.

Put yourself in the shoes of extraterrestrial intelligence and consider what that means. If you were a trillion times smarter than a human being, would you notice the human race at all? Or if you did, would you care? After all, do you notice the 100 trillion microbes or more in your body? No, unless they happen to give you health problems, like E. coli and other sicknesses. More on that later.

One of the big problems with our understandings of aliens has to do with Hollywood. Movies and television have led us to think of aliens as green, slimy creatures traveling around in flying saucers. Nonsense. I think if advanced aliens have just 100 years more evolution than us, they almost certainly won't be static physical beings anymore—at least not in the molecular sense. They also won't be artificial intelligences living in machines either, which is what I believe humans are evolving into this century. No, becoming machine intelligence is just another passing phase of evolution—one that might only last a few decades for humans, if that.

Truly advanced intelligence will likely be organized intelligently on the atomic scale, and likely even on scales far smaller. Aliens will evolve until they are pure, willful conscious energy—and maybe even something beyond that. They long ago realized that biology and ones and zeroes in machines was literally too rudimentary to be very functional. True advanced intelligence will be spirit-like—maybe even like people's ideas of ghosts.

On a long enough time horizon, every biological species would at some point evolve into machines, and then evolve into intelligent energy with a consciousness. Such brilliant life might have the ability to span millions of lights years nearly instantaneously throughout the universe, morphing into whatever form it wanted.

Like all evolving life, the key to attaining the highest form of being and intelligence possible was to intimately become and control the best universal elements—those that are conducive to such goals, especially personal power over nature. Everything else in advanced alien evolution is discarded as nonfunctional and nonessential.

All intelligence in the universe, like all matter and energy, follows patterns—based on rules of physics. We engage—and often battle—those patterns and rules, until we understand them, and utilize them as best as possible. Such is evolution. And the universe is imbued with wanting life to arise and evolve, as MIT physicist Jeremy England, points out in his *Quanta Magazine* article titled *A New Physics Theory of Life*.

Back to my ant collector friend in Western Samoa. It would be nice to believe that the difference between the ant collector and the ant's intelligence was the same between humans and very sophisticated aliens. Sadly, that is not the case. Not even close.

The difference between a species that has just 75 more years of evolution than us could be a billion times that of an ant versus a human—given the acceleration of intelligence. Now consider an added billion years of evolution. This is way beyond comparing apples and oranges.

The crux of the problem with aliens and humans is we're not hearing or seeing them because we don't have ways to understand their language. It's simply beyond our comprehension and physical abilities. Millions of singularities have already happened, but we're similar to blind bacteria in our bodies running around cluelessly.

The good news, though, is we're about to make contact with the best of the aliens out there. Or rather they're about to school us. The reason: The universe is precious, and in approximately a century's time, humans may be able to conduct physics experiments that could level the entire universe—such as building massive particle accelerators that make the God particle swallow the cosmos whole.

Like a grumpy landlord at the door, alien intelligence will make contact and let us know what we can and can't do when it comes to messing with the real estate of the universe. Knock. Knock.

****

4) Singularity or Transhumanism: What Word Should We Use to Discuss the Future?

Singularity. Posthuman. Techno-Optimism, Cyborgism. Humanity+. Immortalist. Machine intelligence. Biohacker. Robotopia. Life extension. Transhumanism.

These are all terms thrown around trying to describe a future in which mind uploading, indefinite lifespans, artificial intelligence, and bionic augmentation may (and I think will) help us to become far more than just human. They are words you hear in a MIT robotics laboratory, or on a launch site of SpaceX, or on Reddit's Futurology channel.

This word war is a clash of intellectual ideals. It goes something like this: The singularity people (many at Singularity University) don't like the term transhumanism. Transhumanists don't like posthumanism. Posthumanists don't like cyborgism. And cyborgism advocates don't like the life extension tag. If you arrange the groups in any order, the same enmity occurs. All sides are wary of others, fearing they might lose ground in bringing the future closer in precisely their way.

While there is overlap, each name represents a unique camp of thought, strategy, and possible historical outcome for the people pushing their vision of the future. Whatever wins out will be the buzzword that both the public and history will embrace as we continue to move into a future rife with uncertainty and risk, one where for the first time in history, the human being may no longer be classified as a mammal.

For much of the last 30 years, the battle of the best futurist buzzword was fought in science fiction literature and television. Star Trek popularized borg—which helped give commonly used cyborg its meaning. Various short stories and novels tell tales of posthuman civilizations.

The last 15 years marked a shift toward nonfiction work and following of celebrity scientists. Ray Kurzweil's book *The Singularity Is Near* put the term singularity prominently on the word battle map. Biogerontologist Aubrey de Grey's many public appearances touting medical discoveries to conquer human death did the same for life extension science (also called longevity research or the anti-aging field).

The word transhumanism has also long been in use, pushed by philosophers like Max More, David Pearce, and Nick Bostrom. However, until recently, it remained mostly a cult word, used by smaller futurist associations, tech blogs, and older male academics interested in describing radical technology revolutionizing the human experience. Two years ago, a Google search of the word transhumanism—which literally means beyond human—brought up about 100,000 pages. What a difference a few years makes. Today, the word transhumanism now returns almost 2 million pages on Google. And dozens of large social media groups on Facebook and Google+—consisting of every type of race, age group, sexual orientation, heritage, religion, and nationality—have transhuman in their titles. It's also the term that I'm backing, even though I'm not sure it will win out.

Why did this happen so quickly? As with the evolution of most movements and their names, there were numerous moving parts. Dan Brown's international best-seller novel *The Inferno* introduced millions of people to transhumanism. So have media celebrities as diverse as Joe Rogan, Glenn Beck, and Jason Silva, host of National Geographic's *Brain Games*—all three have discussed transhumanism in their work. Even my own relentless writings of transhumanism at search engine-dominating *Huff Post* and *Vice* have helped. A larger reason probably was that both the public and media were ready for an impactful, straightforward word to describe the general flavor of technological existence sweeping over the human race. In case you haven't noticed, the dead live via saline cooling suspended animation, the handicapped walk via exoskeleton technology, and the deaf hear via brain microchip implants. The age of frequent, life-altering science is now upon us, and transhumanism is the most functional word to describe it.

Even though the words singularity, cyborg, and life extension generate more hits on Google than transhumanism, they just don't feel right describing an ideal and accurate vision of the future. Few people are willing to call themselves a Singularitarian—someone who advocates for a technological event that involves a helpful superintelligence. And Cyborgism is just weird, since the public isn't ready to be merged with machines yet. Life extension isn't bad, but it's generally limited only to living longer.

Almost by default, transhumanism has become the overwhelming leader of the name rivalry. Around the world, a quickly growing number of people know what transhumanism is and also subscribe to some of it. It has become the go-to futurist term to express how science and technology are upending the human playing field.

****

5) Capitalism 2.0: The Economy of the Future Will be Powered by Neural Prosthetics

A battle for the "soul" of the global economy is underway. The next few decades will likely decide whether capitalism survives or is replaced with a techno-fuelled quasi-socialism where robots do most of the jobs while humans live off government support, likely a designated guaranteed or basic income.

Many experts believe wide-scale automation is inevitable. Even the world's largest hedge fund, Bridgewater Associates, recently announced it's building an AI to replace its managers, many of whom are highly educated and previously thought invulnerable to automation. Robots, it seems, will manage everything. Or will they?

A next-generation technology, likely to arrive in five to 10 years, is being credited as the savior of capitalism. Known today as neural prosthetics, or neural lace, it's essentially tech that reads your brainwaves. This tech promises to connect our brains to the cloud and AI to link us with machines using thought alone.

While this technology sounds farfetched, hundreds of thousands of people globally have implants connected to their brains. Up till now, all of them have been implanted for medical reasons, with the most common being the cochlear implant which allows the deaf to hear by stimulating the auditory nerve. Increasingly, patients with Parkinson's and Alzheimer's are testing out the technology in the hope of staving off their diseases. And President Obama's BRAIN initiative, announced in 2013, allocated $70 million to government-funded DARPA to jumpstart the field of brain implants.

For humans to beat the machines, or at least be competitive, we're going to have to follow this path; to connect with them directly.

One California startup founded by entrepreneur Bryan Johnson is called Kernel. Kernel wants to build a neural prosthetic that would allow humans, among other things, to keep up with the machines in real time, similar to a human mind literally being connected to the internet and all its algorithms and search functions.

Elsewhere, Elon Musk recently announced plans to start a neural lace company called Neuralink. Known for making wild tech bets, Musk said in Dubai, in March: "Over time I think we will probably see a closer merger of biological intelligence and digital intelligence." In particular, he hopes to have success with his new company in just five years' time.

The challenging reality suggests that if humans don't develop these implants or headsets, hundreds of millions of jobs will be lost to robots. Some, like myself, even believe Wall Street will be emptied of human traders. The same automation takeover will also likely hit law offices, engineering firms, and even politicians might one day be replaced by machines that seek only to help the people through the best, most altruistic algorithms.

Neural prosthetics will eliminate that. It will preserve competition – not only in the human race, but against machines. For those, like me, who appreciate most parts of capitalism and what it's done for progress and innovation, that's a good thing.

But it'll take more than just a mind tapped into the cloud to be widely competitive in the overall job market. Augmented limbs, bionic organs, and widespread use of exoskeleton technology will be needed to compete against robotic strength.

For years I've been supportive of a basic income, which would provide a monthly income for the poor – mostly because I saw it as the only logical way to keep people fed and housed, while still allowing for technological and economic evolution. Now, with neural prosthetics and upgraded bodies, I see the future may, instead, be full of capitalistic enterprise, fueled by transhumanist technologies that allow us to more closely resemble the machines.

That's not to say I'm abandoning my views on basic income. Instead, I believe there will be another aspect to the future economy that isn't only for the robot and AI manufacturers, but for hundreds of millions – maybe billions – of people willing to use tech to compete against machines. A future motto of humanity and capitalism might be: "If you can't beat a machine, become one." As a radical science and technology advocate, that's a philosophy I can support.

****

6) Genetic Editing Could Cause World War III

While *Time* magazine recently chose President-Elect Donald Trump as its Person of the Year, CRISPR gene editing pioneers were a runner-up choice. Few innovations in the last millennium carry such transformative prospects as the ability to edit our own genome and make ourselves into fundamentally something else. Some experts think genetic editing might be the key to curing all disease and achieving perfect health.

Unlike other epic scientific advances—like the 1945 explosion of the first atomic bomb in New Mexico—the immediate effect of genetic editing technology is not dangerous. Yet, it stands to be just as divisive to humans as the 70-year proliferation of nuclear weaponry. On one hand, you have secular-minded China and its scientists leading the gene editing revolution, openly modifying the human genome in hopes of improving the human being. On the other hand, you have a broadly Republican US administration and Congress that appears to be strongly Christian—conservatives who often insist humans should remain just as God created them.

Therein lies a great coming conflict, one that I'm sure will lead to street protests, riots, and civil strife—the kind described explicitly in my novel *The Transhumanist Wager*, where a religious-fundamentalist government shuts down extreme science in the name of conservatism. The playing field of geopolitics is pretty simple: If China or another country vows to increase its children's intelligence via genetic editing (which I estimate they will be able to do in 6-12 years time), and America chooses to remain "au naturel" because they insist that's how God made them, a conflict species-deep will quickly arise. If this scenario seems too bizarre to happen, just consider the Russian Olympic track and field team that was banned in the recent 2016 Games for supposed doping.

It's quite possible the same accusatory flavor of "banning" could happen between China and America in the game of life—between its workers, its politicians, is people, its artists, and its media. I wonder if America—approximately 70 percent who identify as Christians—will put up with beings who modified themselves by science to be smarter and more functional entities.

This type of idea takes racism and immigration to a whole new level. Will America close off its borders, its jobs, its schools, and its general openness to the world to stay pure, old-fashioned human? Will we stop trading, befriending, and even starting families with those who are modified?

In short, will genetic editing start a new cold war? One that bears much finger pointing and verbal reprimands, including the use of derogatory terms like mutants, cyborgs, and transhumanists. Think the videogame Dues Ex, but with modified people taking all the best jobs. In a worst-case scenario, it could even start a World War.

So, now that we know what can happen if America won't embrace the most important science to emerge this century, how can we avoid it?

First—and this is wishful thinking, since 100 percent of the US Congress and the Supreme Court appear to be religious at the moment—is we could just embrace genetic editing and be better at it than the Chinese. This is the exact scenario I suggest. Yes, it will lead to a place where beings are similar to those in Star Wars and Star Trek, but after all, we love those stories because we want to reach that super-science age. And in the long run, such evolution of the species is inevitable anyway, so long as we don't kill ourselves first in a nuclear war or an environmental catastrophe.

In a second scenario, America could focus more on technology and less on biology and genetics. On my recent 4-month long Immortality Bus tour across America, I found conservative people seem more inclined to use tech accessories or wear a special headset that would make them smarter (for example, by connecting their thoughts Matrix-style into the cloud and AI)—as opposed to structurally changing their brains, as the Chinese likely will do. America could innovate that accessory tech that would keep us ahead of the biological modifications of other nations. I'll accept that—reluctantly—if the first scenario I presented is a no-go.

A third way—and this is the blatant transhumanist nightmare—is we could establish a non-modification policy across all countries, similar to how we have created the Paris Treaty for climate change or rules of war that ban chemical weapons. The major nations of the world, sensing a significant global legal issue in genetic editing, could come together as a species and criminalize the science.

To some extent, this has already happened, because as soon as the world realized the Chinese had experimented on the human genome, calls were made to put a stop on some of this science. Such a reaction is not dissimilar from what George W. Bush did with stem cells when his religious values made him shut down federal funding on all but a tiny portion of the research in America. Stem cells have since been shown to be one of the most important medical applications in the world, and those lost years of science have potentially negatively affected millions of lives.

Sadly, the third option of a general or even partial moratorium on genetic editing will surely harm innovation. The great thing with gene editing is we can likely do many wondrous things with it, such as potentially cure cancer, halt aging, grow better organs, and overcome disability by better repairing ourselves. Beyond making ourselves superhuman, we can simply make ourselves better fit for Earth, including dealing with a changing environment.

I also don't think the third option will work in the long run. More than ever, science is the hands of individuals, who can buy amazing biotesting kits on eBay for just a $1000—as well as incredibly powerful computers to analyze the data. Citizen scientists would just create the new gene editing tech and begin doing it themselves—perhaps more dangerously had the government not been overseeing the research from the start.

I argue for the first path. Let's allow good, old-fashioned scientific competition with China to proceed. Let's see which country can create the best enhancements for their citizenry, and let's share the best of our work with one another in the end to make it so all peoples are as equal as possible. If we're too closed-minded about such radical science, we might find ourselves embroiled in a state of hostile speciation, where another new cold war—or worse—swallows a generation.

****

7) What If One Country Achieves the Singularity First?

The concept of a technological singularity is tough to wrap your mind around. Even experts have differing definitions. Vernor Vinge, responsible for spreading the idea in the 1990s, believes it's a moment when growing superintelligence renders our human models of understanding obsolete. Google's Ray Kurzweil says it's "a future period during which the pace of technological change will be so rapid, its impact so deep, that human life will be irreversibly transformed." *Gizmodo* Editor-in-Chief Annalee Newitz explained, "A good way to understand the singularity is to imagine explaining the internet to somebody living in the year 1200." Even Christian theologians have chimed in, sometimes referring to it as "the rapture of the nerds."

My own definition of the singularity is: the point where a fully functioning human mind radically and exponentially increases its intelligence and possibilities via physically merging with technology.

All these definitions share one basic premise—that technology will speed up the acceleration of intelligence to a point when biological human understanding simply isn't enough to comprehend what's happening anymore.

That also makes a technological singularity something quasi-spiritual, since anything beyond understanding evokes mystery. It's worth noting that even most naysayers and luddites who disdain the singularity concept don't doubt that the human race is heading towards it.

In March 2015, I published a *Vice Motherboard* article titled *A Global Arms Race to Create a Superintelligent AI is Looming*. The article argued a concept I call the AI Imperative, which says that nations should do all they can to develop artificial intelligence, because whichever country produces an AI first will likely end up ruling the world indefinitely, since that AI will be able to control all other technologies and their development on the planet.

The article generated many thoughtful comments on Reddit Futurology, LessWrong, and elsewhere. I tend not to comment on my own articles in an effort to stay out of the way, but I do always carefully read comment sections. One thing the message boards on this story made me think about was the possibility of a "nationalistic" singularity—what might also be called an exclusive or private singularity.

If you're a technophile like me, you probably believe the key to reaching the singularity is two-fold: the creation of a superintelligence, and the ability to merge humans with that intelligence. Without both, it's probably impossible for people to reach it. With both, it's probably inevitable.

Currently, the technology to merge the human brain with a machine is already underway. In fact, hundreds of thousands of people around the world already have brain implants of some sort, and a few years ago telepathy was performed between researchers in different countries. Thoughts were passed from one mind to another using a machine interface, without speaking a word.

Fast forward 25 years in the future, and some experts believe we might already be able to upload our entire consciousness into a machine. I tend to agree, and I even think it could occur sooner, such as in 15 to 20 years' time.

Here's the crux: If an AI exclusively belonged to one nation (which is likely to happen), and the technology of merging human brains and machines grows sufficiently (which is also likely to happen), then you could possibly end up with one nation controlling the pathways into the singularity.

As insane as this sounds, it's possible that the controlling nation could start offering its citizens the opportunity to be uploaded fully into machines, in preparation to enter the singularity. Whether there would then be two distinct entities—one biological and one uploaded—for every human who chooses to do this is a natural question, and it's only one that could be decided at the time, probably by governments and law. Furthermore, once uploaded, would your digital self be able to interact with your biological self? Would one self be able to help the other? Or would laws force an either-or situation, where uploaded people's biological selves must remain in cryogenically frozen states or even be eliminated altogether?

No matter how you look at this, it's bizarre futurist stuff. And it presents a broad array of challenging ethical issues, since some technologists see the singularity as something akin to a totally new reality or even a so-called digital heaven. And to have one nation or government controlling it, or even attempting to limit it exclusively to its populace, seems potentially morally dubious.

For example, what if America created the AI first, then used its superintelligence to pursue a singularity exclusively for Americans?

(Historically, this wouldn't be that far off from what many Abrahamic world religions advocate for, such as Christianity or Islam. In both religions, only certain types of people get to go to heaven. Those left behind get tortured for eternity. This concept of exclusivity is the single largest reason I turned nonreligious when I was 18 years-old.)

Worse, what if a government chose only to allow the super wealthy to pursue its doorway to the singularity—to plug directly into its superintelligent AI? Or what if the government only gave access to high-ranked party officials? For example, how would Russia's Vladimir Putin deal with this type of power? And it is a tremendous power. After all, you'd be connected to a superintelligence and would likely be able to rewrite all the nuclear arms codes in the world, stop dams and power plants from operating, and create a virus to shut down Wi-Fi worldwide, if you wanted.

Of course, given the option, many people would probably choose not to undergo the singularity at all. I suspect many would choose to remain as they are on Earth. However, some of those people might be keen on acquiring the technology of getting to the singularity. They might want to sell that tech, and offer paid one-way trips for people who want to have a singularity. For that matter, individuals or corporations might try to patent it. What you'd be selling is the path to vast amounts of power and immortality.

Such moral leanings and concepts that someone or group could control, patent, or steal the singularity ultimately lead us to another imperative: the Singularity Disparity.

The first person or group to experience the singularity will protect and preserve the power and intelligence they've acquired in the singularity process—which ultimately means they will do whatever is necessary to lessen the power and intelligence accumulation of the singularity experience for others. That way the original Singularitarians can guarantee their power and existence indefinitely.

In my philosophical novel *The Transhumanist Wager*, this type of thinking belongs to the Omnipotender, someone who is actively seeking and contending for as much power as possible, and bases their actions on such endeavors.

I'm not trying to argue any of this is good or bad, moral or immoral. I'm just explaining how this phenomena of the singularity likely could unfold. Assuming I'm correct, and technology continues to grow rapidly, the person who will become the leading omnipotender on Earth is already born.

Of course, religions will appreciate that fact, because such a person will fulfill elements of either the Antichrist or the Second Coming of a Jesus, which is important to both the apocalyptic beliefs in Christianity and Islam. At least the "End Times" are really here, faith-touters will be able to finally say.

The good news, though, is that maybe a singularity is not an exclusive event. Maybe there can be many singularities.

A singularity is likely to be mostly a consciousness phenomenon. We will be nearly all digital and interconnected with machines, but we will still able to recognize ourselves, values, memories, and our purposes—otherwise I don't think we'd go through with it. On the cusp of the singularity, our intelligence will begin to grow tremendously. I expect the software of our minds will be able to be rewritten and upgraded almost instantaneously in real time. I also think the hardware we exist through—whatever form of computing it'll be—will also be able to be reshaped and remade in real time. We'll learn how to reassemble processors and their particles in the moment, on-demand, probably with the same agility and speed we have when thinking about something, such as figuring out a math problem. We'll understand the rules and think about what we want, and the best answer, strategy, and path will occur. We'll get exceedingly efficient at such things, too. And at some point, we won't see a difference between matter, energy, judgment, and ourselves.

What's important here is the likely fact that we won't care much about what's left on Earth. In just days or even hours, the singularity will probably render us into some form of energy that can organize and advance itself superintelligently, perhaps into a trillion minds on a million Earths.

If the singularity occurs like this, then, on the surface, there's little ethically wrong with a national or private singularity, because other nations or groups could implement their own in time. However, the larger issue is: How would people on Earth protect themselves from someone or some group in the singularity who decides the Earth and its inhabitants aren't worth keeping around, or worse, wants to enslave everyone on Earth? There's no easy answer to this, but the question itself makes me frown upon the singularity idea, in exactly the same way I frown upon an omnipotent God and heaven. I don't like any other single entity or group having that much possible power over another.

****

8) Why I'm Running for President as the Transhumanist Candidate

It's a wild request to ask a nation to consider electing you as their president, especially when you're a transhumanist—someone who advocates for using science and technology to radically change and improve the human species. But I'm doing it.

In October 2014, I declared my 2016 US candidacy under the newly formed Transhumanist Party, which I founded, and promised my community of techno-optimists I'd do everything I could to use my campaign as a way to speed up the arrival of robotic hearts, brain implants, artificial limbs, exoskeleton suits, and indefinite lifespans—all of which are just a small part of the radical science transhumanists aim to make a standard part of people's lives.

The Transhumanist Party may seem fringe to some, but it's not. It's mainly made up of scientists, engineers, futurists, and people who love technology. And while we don't have a formal paying membership process, my officers and I estimate—based on social media, event turnouts, and donations—we now have about 25,000 supporters in the US. We also have approximately 40 volunteers and more signing up every week. Globally, there are now almost 25 Transhumanist Parties on five different continents, each with its own rules that it determines best within its national framework.

My presidential campaign has been nothing short of a whirlwind. Take this morning for example. I woke up to my iPad beeping relentlessly with inbound messages—dozens of emails, Facebook posts, and tweets asking my policies on everything from artificial wombs, to a proposed moratorium on AI research, to the Baltimore riots. After brewing coffee, I answered as many requests as I could.

Later, I began the tedious business of negotiating a reality TV contract on my campaign. After taking my 4-year-old daughter to preschool, I returned to my desk and typed up a blog post supporting Chinese scientists editing the genome, then put together my slideshow for an upcoming speech in Vancouver, then worked with a designer on the Transhumanist Party's latest bumper sticker.

Finally, I spent a half-hour checking out bus companies for my campaigns summer bus tour, scheduled to start this July on the West Coast.

By noon I was almost caught up on most urgent campaign matters and starting to look forward to my mid-day jog when the flow was broken by one my communications managers asking how I planned to answer inquiring press on 3D-printed guns. This is a sticky issue.

Generally, transhumanists love anything 3D-printed—especially when it concerns human organs and bionics—but the question at hand was whether manufacturing a lethal weapon is going too far, especially when anyone could do it by buying a 3D-printer off Ebay for a under $2000?

Guns play an integral part in thousands of accidental deaths, murders, and armed robberies every year in America, so the ability to quickly, cheaply, and anonymously make them in your home or even in your car is highly contentious. I generally advocate for giving people nearly all liberties, but I had no idea how to delicately answer this question, and neither did any of my staff. An advisor said we should check out what the US Constitution's Second Amendment (the right to bear arms) said about 3D-printers. We laughed, thinking it ridiculous to try governing a country with a 226-year old document in the transhumanist age.

People ask me all the time—since they know I'm not going to win the presidency (third party candidates never win)—if I'm enjoying the campaign. I've never thought about it like that.

I've only focused on one thing through it all—the same thing I've focused on with all my work for much of the last decade: I don't want to die. Like most transhumanists, it's not that I'm afraid of death, but I emphatically believe being alive is a miracle. Out of two billion planets that might have life in the universe, human beings managed to evolve, survive, and thrive on Planet Earth—enough so the species will probably reach the singularity in a half century's time and literally become superhuman.

The whole experience of life is crazy and beautiful and precious. We need to protect and preserve that life, at all costs. The only rational way one can do that is with technology and science, which is exactly the principle the Transhumanist Party was formed upon. Transhumanists are a people defined specifically by their love of life.

I've been lucky and grateful that so many people agree with me. Renowned gerontologist Aubrey de Grey has recently signed on as my Anti-aging Advisor. Millennial entrepreneur Riva-Melissa Tez is my Strategy Advisor. Jose Cordeiro, PhD, faculty at Singularity University, is my Technology Advisor. Former Democratic Congressional candidate Gabriel Rothblatt, son of transgendered billionaire entrepreneur Martine Rothblatt is my political advisor.

Even my wife, Dr. Lisa Memmel, a women's rights advocate and an ObGyn at Planned Parenthood, is a big supporter and member of my campaign. Together we are hoping to change the world and usher in an age where science, technology, and the right to do with your body what you want are not at odds with American culture.

Unfortunately, on many counts, transhumanism is at odds with our national culture. With an American population that is approximately 75% Christian and a US congress almost 100% religious, accomplishing my goal is no easy feat. Most Americans just don't care about the goals of transhumanism. Many subscribe to what I call a "deathist" culture, where they insist we must follow the rules of the Bible, die, and go to heaven to meet Jesus.

As an outspoken atheist (and apparently America's first visible atheist presidential candidate), none of this makes any sense to me. Despite this, I still insist my campaign and the Transhumanist Party welcome all religions and try to be respectful and open-minded of people's beliefs. After all, transhumanism is possibly the least discriminatory philosophy out there—it accepts anyone who wants to be a part of it.

None of this has calmed some of my detractors, though. Some people are downright livid about my ideas and campaign. I've even heard some Christian theologians suggest I might be the antichrist. As ludicrous as this talk is to me and others, it has prompted me to recently buy a bulletproof vest for public speeches. My share of hate email and death threats on Twitter are constant enough to warrant such measures.

These things dampen my spirit in multiple ways, since one of the central goals of the Transhumanist Party and my campaign is to advocate for taking money away from wars, violent activities, and defense, and instead put those resources into medicine to improve health, prosperity, and happiness for the citizenry. Violence, division, discrimination, and deliberately causing conflict are simply not on the transhumanist agenda whatsoever.

Transhumanism is a social movement, like environmentalism, that aims to unite people in a single direction and approach—an approach that is backed up by recent various reports showing that the world is getting better for all people. Over the last 30 years, science and technology have helped reduce infant mortality rates, given everyone longer lives, produced more jobs, lessened wars, improved general health, and made the world a better place. It makes sense then, to speed up the process of technological progress and embrace the transhumanist age, given how it improves lives.

Of course, when looked at it that way, not all Americans are philosophically opposed to transhumanism. And I think with the right diplomacy and gentle nudging, many more people in the states would come on board to embrace transhumanism. With that in mind, I'm on the lookout for new supporters. Aside from science and technology enthusiasts—those who make up the foundation of the Transhumanist Party—I am trying to acquire a new base of supporters that may allow transhumanism to break into mainstream politics.

My 2016 campaign strategy is to target three specific groups: atheists, LGBT people, and the disabled community. Collectively, they number about around 30 million Americans, and some of them are already present in large numbers in the transhumanist community and share similar values. I want to reach supporters of science and technology, and the main philosophical premise of morphological freedom—that you have the right to do with your body whatever you want so long as it doesn't hurt someone else.

Unlike the other Democratic and Republican presidential hopefuls, my campaign is not very technically political. Sure, I try to address questions on taxes, social security, international relations, and other typical candidate topics when asked, but I'm not trying to be spew political ideologies or subscribe to a political party. I don't care about leaning left or right, nor does most of the Transhumanist Party. We're here to offer the kind of change that affects society's entire existence and our rapidly evolving future. We want to convince government and people that a transhumanist-inspired country will not only benefit all, but be an exciting step for the human race.

For example, transhumanists want to reignite the space industry and send citizens all over solar system. We want to build massive seasteading projects where all flavors of people and scientific experimentation can abound. We want to create an artificial superintelligence that can teach us to fix all the environmental problems humans have caused. We want to declare war on cancer, Alzheimer's, and aging—not on drugs, disenfranchised minorities, or small oil-dependent nations.

We want to close economic inequality by establishing a universal basic income and also make education free to everyone at all levels, including college and preschool. We want to reimagine the American Dream, one where robots take our jobs, but we live a life of leisure, exploration, and anything we want on the back of the fruits of 21st Century progress.

My presidential campaign is a strange, tumultuous endeavor to undertake, knowing I have almost zero chance of winning the 2016 election. But I have my sights on other important tasks: growing the Transhumanist Party, developing policies that unite the nation under one techno-optimistic vision, and getting everyday people to desire unlimited lifespans via science. These are important jobs, and this is where my heart and mind are focused daily as I sojourn on the bumpy campaign trail.

****

9) Transhumanist Olympics: Embrace Performance-enhancing Drugs and Technology in Sport

The 2016 Paralympics in Rio de Janeiro is bringing together 4,500 athletes to compete in 23 sports from wheelchair fencing to swimming to hand biking.

In the Paralympics, technology sometimes plays a powerful role. Consider South African sprinter Oscar Pistorius, whose custom-made blades attached to his knees allowed him to win gold at the 2004 and 2008 Paralympics. His prosthetics were improved, and he successfully competed in the 2012 Olympic Games.

In the future, tech improving an athlete's competitive levels will likely dramatically accelerate. After all, technology grows exponentially and humanity has never been so affected by innovation. In fact, it's quite possible exoskeleton suits will be used in sporting events, including track and field. Perhaps within a decade, Paralympians — some quadriplegics — may sprint faster and jump farther than their Olympian counterparts. A paraplegic opened the 2014 World Cup by kicking a soccer ball with his exoskeleton suit on.

Such use of technology and innovation will radically change sports. For this reason, I advocate for creating a Transhumanist Olympics — Games that emphasize the use of tech and science for performance, not just human athleticism.

A Transhumanist Olympics would in some ways mimic Formula One racing, where the technology can be just as important as the driver. This sort of human competition would raise engineers and scientists — not just winning athletes — to the level of superstars. A Transhumanist Olympics would always be a team-oriented competition, even in individual events.

What sports would a Transhumanist Olympics have? Probably many of the ones we have now. The difference would be the addition of radical technology and performance enhancing drugs. And the dramatic lack of rules or regulation.

Sports has become a minefield of regulation and drug use (and paranoia of that drug use). But there's another way — one that doesn't betray us because the use of all competitive advantages is encouraged.

We need a Transhumanist Olympics because it would make competition more interesting. And given NBC's poor TV ratings in Rio — especially with Millennials — this might be just the workout the sporting industry needs.

Take power lifting. Steroids are disallowed in normal competition. So are adrenalin-like shots and other short-term energy boosters, which can give humans extra strength for a limited time. But who doesn't want to see a human being with all the tools of medicine and science lift twice what a natural person could? And why should we breathe during swimming competitions (which slows us down) when we can take injections of oxygen particles that might enable us to hold our breath for the entire 200-meter freestyle?

After the Rio Paralympics, the first Cybathon will be held in October in Switzerland, where bionic and augmented human beings — some without limbs — will compete. It's a forerunner to the kind of sporting event I'm imagining.

The transhumanist age—where radical science and technology make us superhumans—is already here. But so far, no one seems willing to give it a chance when it involves the human body's athleticism. That should change because we already are in an era where it's not who we are, but what we can become through the tools we create — such as driverless cars, smartphones and chip implants. We owe it to ourselves to try this out, and in doing so create a new culture — one that's doesn't shun improvement through radical innovation, but embraces it.

****

CHAPTER II: EARLY WRITINGS: THE PROVACATEUR

10) A World Future Society Conference Speech: Everyone Faces a Transhumanist Wager

Recently, I had the honor to give a speech at the World Futurist Society's conference in Orlando, Florida. My talk at the conference was loosely based on an essay I recently wrote titled *Everyone Faces a Transhumanist Wager*. I wanted to share a condensed version of the talk because it presents a fundamental dilemma every human being on the planet must confront. Here's the shortened speech:

Ladies and gentlemen, we have a problem. Each one of us has a problem. In fact, no matter where you go on the planet, no matter who you find, every single person on Earth has this same dire problem.

That problem is our mortality. That problem is called death.

The reason it's a problem is because human beings love life. We all love the precious chance of existence. Even in one's darkest psychological despair, or one's most exhausting hardship, or one's most catastrophic tragedy, the thing we call life is still always miraculous. We cherish life and we don't want to lose it or have it end.

But end it will. No matter how much we wish otherwise. The stark truth is right before our eyes—that nothing in today's world can save us from death. The obviousness of this overwhelms us every time we see a loved one or a friend whose body is lifeless, never to reach out, touch, and communicate with us again. Death is final.

The great irony for our species is that we don't just have this one problem—but two problems. The second problem is nearly as vicious as the first. The second problem is the fact that most people around the world are just not worried about the first problem—they're not worried about dying. They're either religious and have the supposed afterlife all worked out, or they just don't care, or they just don't think conquering human death is possible. Whatever people's reasons, they just don't see the first problem as serious enough to warrant immediate concern—especially in a meaningful, tangible way that makes them not die. And by not recognizing death as a problem, many people have no reason to attempt to defeat it.

I have made it a mission in my life to make people aware of these two problems. It is why I wrote my philosophical novel *The Transhumanist Wager*. The concept of the Transhumanist Wager in the book is simple. It explains that in the 21st Century—the age of unprecedented technological innovation—it is a betrayal of ourselves (and the potential of our best selves) to not tackle and solve our two most pressing problems using modern science. More importantly, my book explains how we can solve these two problems.

But first, some of you are asking: What is a transhumanist? What does such a person want? What are the main goals? Some people around the world still don't know what transhumanism means. When explaining the term to people, I find it easiest to use the Latin translation. "Transhuman" literally means: beyond human.

Transhumanist goals are broad and varied, but mostly they revolve around human beings using science and technology to radically improve and enhance themselves, their lives, and society. Transhumanists often concentrate on stopping or reversing aging— we are sometimes called life-extensionists or longevity advocates. Many transhumanists also focus on robotics, bionics, artificial intelligence, biohacking, and other similar fields of study. Transhumanists are often, but not always, nonreligious. They find meaning in their own lives and possibilities, without a divine creator. The philosophies of transhumanism make it possible that in the future—using extreme science and technology—one may become a so-called divine creator if they wanted. In almost all circumstances, transhumanists prefer reason over any other method of understanding to guide themselves in life.

Every transhumanist comes to their own realization of why they feel they are a transhumanist. Each path is unique, personal, and totally different than another. I want to tell you briefly about my path. I was first introduced to transhumanism as a philosophy student attending Columbia University in New York City. For a class assignment, I was told to read a magazine article on some of the recent breakthroughs in cryonics. The article described a small but passionate group of scientists who believed that science and technology would be able to bring frozen patients back to life in the future if they were preserved properly. The article also discussed the transhumanism movement, which it described as a community of reason-based futurists who wanted to use science and technology to improve their lives and live indefinitely. I was deeply intrigued. I finished that article and wanted to know more. I spent the next ten years reading everything I could find on future technologies, human enhancement, and transhumanism.

However, it wasn't until I was in the jungles of the demilitarized zone of Vietnam as a journalist for the National Geographic Channel that I came to dedicate my life to the field of transhumanism—that I came to the powerful conviction that human life should be preserved indefinitely. While in the jungle filming Vietnamese bomb diggers searching the ground for unexploded ordinances to recover and sell, I almost stepped on a partially unburied landmine. My guide pushed me out of the way, and I fell to within a foot of the mine. Tens of thousands have died from landmines in the DMZ in the last forty years, and I was lucky I was not one of them.

For me, nothing was ever the same again after that moment. The landmine incident permanently stamped into my mind how fragile the human body was—how precious our minutes alive on this planet really are. Upon returning to the Unites States, I began writing *The Transhumanist Wager*. The reason I tell you my personal story about becoming a transhumanist is that every one of us has their own story. But the two main problems we each face: death, and general apathy of death—and the choice we must make regarding them: a Transhumanist Wager—that is not just for some people. It is for every reasonable person in the world.

Indeed, in the quickly advancing 21st Century, making a Transhumanist Wager approaches us now as an ultimatum—the most challenging one we may ever face. Luckily, given how fast modern science is growing and changing our lives, making the wager is also the only reasonable option. If you love life, you will dedicate yourself to finding a way to preserve that life. Transhumanists do not want to preserve their life via heaven-promising religions, false hopes, an unconscious mystic super spirituality, or otherwise. There are only rational ways transhumanists will do it: through the tools they can create with their own hands; through the reason their brains can muster; and through the conviction their being prompts of them by not wanting to die and disappear. To do otherwise in today's world is to remain irrational and, as my novel discusses, to be masochistic and even borderline suicidal. In a world where we have the technology to travel to Mars, where we can video chat on our cell phones to someone 10,000 miles away, or we can triple the lifespan of mice with biotechnology, it's our evolutionary destiny to significantly extend our lives and to be transhuman.

Once you have identified the human race's two main problems, and you understand that you each face a Transhumanist Wager, the question is: what to do? How can you solve these problems and make the right choice in the wager?

It's quite simple, really. The journey of the transhumanist requires no ritual, no prayer, and no spiritual sacrifice or payment. It requires only your ability to reason. Ask yourself how you can best dedicate yourself to a specific cause of transhumanism and its various fields: aging research, cyborgology, stem cell science, suspended animation, singularitarianism, genetic engineering, machine intelligence, or the dozens of other areas. Then do it. For some, this may mean going into science or technology as a new career. For others it will mean volunteering in transhuman groups that need support. For some it will mean going into politics and pushing for more science-friendly laws. For others, it will mean donating resources to scientific centers and struggling innovators. For some, it will mean creating transhumanist art and using it a vehicle to push for a more scientific-minded society. For others it will mean just talking with friends and family about why you think science and technology are the best drivers of civilization.

Whatever it is that one can do, be transhumanist-minded. Be a people that belongs to a bright, rational scientific future, not one dogged by the old ways of archaic institutions, apathy, fear, or primitivism. Be transhuman, and let us all embrace our evolutionary destiny and the joys of perfect health and being that science can help us reach.

****

11) Some Futurists Aren't Worried About Global Warming or Overpopulation

It's almost impossible to view the news anymore without seeing something negative related to global warming, overpopulation or environmental degradation of the planet. The facts speak for themselves. Pollution is rampant in many cities. Entire forests are being cut down. And the human species is adding over 200,000 new people a day to the world. Environmental scientists have warned for years that the human race is dramatically affecting the planet and its ecosystems. Humans are changing the climate of Earth, consuming all its finite resources, and causing the disappearance of over 10,000 species a year.

Despite this, a growing number of futurists, many who are transhumanists — people who aim to move beyond the human being using science and technology — aren't worried. While New York City, Boston and Miami may be partially underwater by 2100, many futurists don't plan to be around in the flesh by then. And if they are, they'll have the technology to walk on water. In fact, many futurists believe that before the end of this century, they will become cyborgs, sentient robots, virtual avatars living inside computers, or space travelers journeying on starships in far-off solar systems.

This sounds like science fiction to the general public. However, imagine if you had told someone in 1914 that in 2014 much of the world's population would have access to making video conference calls on handheld wireless devices to people on the other side of the planet. No one would've believed you. After all, how could arrangements of radio waves travel almost instantaneously around the planet and perfectly mirror multiple conversations on the screen of a tiny handheld machine?

What many environmentalists, journalists and politicians fail to consider when assessing the future is how quickly technological innovation is growing. The future is coming much faster than people realize.

According to Moore's Law, the number of transistors on integrated circuits doubles about every 18 months. Technological advancements generally evolve at the same speed too, making the improvement exponential. While Moore's Law may not hold out to be true indefinitely and cannot be used to address all aspects of technological growth, the point that tech innovation is soon to be at Olympic-like speed is well-noted.

As mammals with brains that haven't biologically evolved much in the last 100,000 years, it's hard for many of us to fathom what exponential scientific and technological growth really means. Our brains are wired to perceive life as it occurs, moment to moment. We're very good at recognizing and jumping away from a poisonous snake in the grass, but not so good at understanding choices and their consequences that take place over a quarter-century. Nonetheless, graphs that chart scientific progress do not lie. We are entering a phase where our technological innovation will spike and continue until we likely reach a Singularity.

This spike of technological growth will bring about a paradigm shift in human existence. Globally, there are dozens of companies and universities working on how to control robotic limbs and parts with brain waves. Already, the U.S. military is successfully experimenting with mind-controlled fighter jets. And humans have already started attempting to download their thoughts into computers. Soon, a software interface will bring to life our authentic virtual personalities. Eventually, especially with the help of artificial intelligence, we will complete a full upload of our brains, and our minds and its thoughts will freely move in and out of machines. We will be digital avatars of our biological selves.

All this begs the question: Will this new phase of human existence require as many resources from the planet as we are currently using? Will we continue to eat food? Breathe air? Depend on water? Procreate? The answer is probably not. There is a time coming in this century when populations of humans will no longer be so dependent on continued usage of the Earth's finite bounty. Achieving a sustainable harmony with nature, while politically correct in today's world, may quickly lose relevance. The fact that so many people are worried about using up all the planet's fossil fuels will soon become silly.

Many environmental and social scientists should realize that forecasts looking forward 50 years are likely to be embarrassingly wrong if they're only focusing on humans. In the future, many people will be transhuman. Entire new forms of being will be created to fulfill needs and desires of our advancing species. To make accurate forecasts, a transhumanist perspective — not a Homo sapiens one — will be necessary. The entire population of the world and all its thoughts, experiences, and forms may one day fit into something the size of Stanley Kubrick's black monolith in the movie 2001: A Space Odyssey. That is where we're heading and how dramatically the species will change.

Until then, the real dangers of human civilization lurk in those who want to hinder or over-regulate progress. Science and technology have brought us a far better world, scoring numerous victories for humanity. Globally, democracy is more widespread than ever, poverty is declining, and the species is healthier and living longer according to various recent reports by the United Nations.

There are probably zero futurists who feel good about damaging our beautiful planet. However, many of them realize that the benefit of the species' rapid evolutionary ascent outweighs the harm progress is causing to Earth. Our planet is strong; it can handle climate change and an expanding human population while our species prepares for the transhumanist age. The evolutionary outcome of humanity will be better for turning a blind eye on Mother Earth. Exponential technological growth, increased prosperity from globalization, and maintaining world peace are the critical issues of the future, not global warming, overpopulation or environmental degradation.

****

12) When Does Hindering Life Extension Science Become a Crime?

Every human being has both a minimum and a maximum amount of life hours left to live. If you add together the possible maximum life hours of every living person on the planet, you arrive at a special number: the optimum amount of time for our species to evolve, find happiness, and become the most that it can be. Many reasonable people feel we should attempt to achieve this maximum number of life hours for humankind. After all, very few people actually wish to prematurely die or wish for their fellow humans' premature deaths.

In a free and functioning democratic society, it's the duty of our leaders and government to implement laws and social strategies to maximize these life hours that we want to safeguard. Regardless of ideological, political, religious, or cultural beliefs, we expect our leaders and government to protect our lives and ensure the maximum length of our lifespans. Any other behavior cuts short the time human beings have left to live. Anything else becomes a crime of prematurely ending human lives. Anything else fits the common legal term we have for that type of reprehensible behavior: criminal manslaughter.

In 2001, former President George W. Bush restricted federal funding for stem cell research, one of the most promising fields of medicine in the 21st Century. Stem cells can be used to help fight disease and, therefore, can lengthen lives. Bush restricted the funding because his conservative religious beliefs—some stem cells came from aborted fetuses—conflicted with his fiduciary duty of helping millions of ailing, disease-stricken human beings. Much medical research in the United States relies heavily on government funding and the legal right to do the research. Ultimately, when a disapproving President limits public resources for a specific field of science, the research in that field slows down dramatically—even if that research would obviously lengthen and improve the lives of millions.

It's not just politicians that are prematurely ending our lives with what can be called "pro-death" policies and ideologies. In 2009, on a trip to Africa, Pope Benedict XVI told journalists that the epidemic of AIDS would be worsened by encouraging people to use condoms. More than 25 million people have died from AIDS since the first cases began being reported in the news in the early 1980s. In numerous studies, condoms have been shown to help stop the spread of HIV, the virus that causes AIDS.

This makes condoms one of the simplest and most affordable life extension tools on the planet. Unfathomably, the billion-person strong Catholic Church actively supports the idea that condom usage is sinful, despite the fact that such a malicious policy has helped sicken and kill a staggering amount of innocent people.

Hank Pellissier, a futurist and organizer of the conference Transhuman Visions, says, "The public majority disapproves of Christian Scientist and Jehovah's Witness parents who deny medicine to children afflicted with life-threatening illness. The public regards the anti-science attitudes of these faiths as unacceptable. Likewise, we should similarly disapprove of the withholding of any medicine or life extension practices that deter death for individuals, of any age."

Regrettably, in 2014, America continues to be permeated with an anti-life extension culture. Genetic engineering experiments in humans often have to pass numerous red-tape-laden government regulatory bodies in order to conduct any tests at all, especially at publicly funded universities and research centers. Additionally, many states still ban human reproductive cloning, which could one day play a critical part in extending human life. The current US administration is also culpable. The White House is simply not doing enough to extend American lifespans. The US Government spends just 2% of the national budget on science and medical research, while their defense budget is over 20%, according to a 2011 US Office of Management Budget chart. Does President Obama not care about this fact, or is he unaware that not actively funding and supporting life extension research indeed shortens lives?

In my philosophical novel *The Transhumanist Wager*, there is a scene which takes place outside of a California courthouse where transhumanist activists are holding up a banner. The words inscribed on the banner sum up key data:

By not actively funding life extension research, the amount of life hours the United States Government is stealing from its citizens is thousands of times more than all the American life hours lost in the Twin Towers tragedy, the AIDS epidemic, and the Vietnam War combined. Demand that your government federally fund transhuman research, nullify anti-science laws, and promote a life extension culture. The average human body can be made to live healthily and productively beyond age 150.

Some longevity experts think that with a small amount of funding—$50 billion dollars—targeted specifically towards life extension research and ending human mortality, average human lifespans could be increased by 25-50 years in about a decade's time. The world's net worth is over $200 trillion dollars, so the species can easily spare a fraction of its wealth to gain some of the most valuable commodities humans have: health and time.

Unfortunately, our species has already lost a massive amount of life hours; billions of lives have been unnecessarily cut short in the last 50 years because of widespread anti-science attitudes and policies. Even in the modern 21st Century, our evolutionary development continues to be significantly hampered by world leaders and governments who believe in non-empirical, faith-driven religious doctrines—most of which require the worship of deities whose teachings totally negate the need for radical life extension science. Virtually every major leader on the planet believes their "God" will give them an afterlife in a heavenly paradise, so living longer on planet Earth is just not that important.

Back in the real world, 150,000 people died yesterday. Another 150,000 will cease to exist today, and the same amount will disappear tomorrow. A good way to reverse this widespread deathist attitude should start with investigative government and non-government commissions examining whether public fiduciary duty requires acting in the best interest of people's health and longevity. Furthermore, investigative commissions should be set up to examine whether former and current top politicians and religious leaders are guilty of shortening people's lives for their own selfish beliefs and ideologies. Organizations and other global leaders that have done the same should be scrutinized and investigated too. And if fault or crimes against humanity are found, justice should be administered. After all, it's possible that the Catholic Church's stance on condoms will be responsible for more deaths in Africa than the Holocaust was responsible for in Europe. Over one million AIDS victims died in Africa last year alone. Catholicism is growing quickly in Africa, and there will soon be nearly 200 million Catholics on the continent.

As a civilization of advanced beings who desire to live longer, better, and more successfully, it is our responsibility to put government, religious institutions, big business, and other entities that endorse pro-death policies on notice. Society should stand ready to prosecute anyone that deliberately promotes agendas and actions that prematurely end people's useful lives. Stifling or hindering life extension science, education, and practices needs to be recognized as a legitimate crime.

****

13) The Morality of Artificial Intelligence and the Three Laws of Transhumanism

I recently gave a speech at the *Artificial Intelligence and The Singularity* conference in Oakland, California. My speech topic was "The Morality of an Artificial Intelligence Will be Different from our Human Morality."

Recently, entrepreneur Elon Musk made major news when he warned on Twitter that AI could be "potentially more dangerous than nukes." A few days later, a journalist asked me to respond to his statement, and I answered:

The coming of artificial intelligence will likely be the most significant event in the history of the human species. Of course, it can go badly, as Elon Musk warned recently. However, it can just as well catapult our species to new and unimaginable transhumanist heights. Within a few months of the launch of an artificial intelligence equal or smarter than humans, expect nearly every science and technology book to be completely rewritten with new ideas — better and far more complex ideas. Expect a new era of learning and advanced life for our species. The key, of course, is not to let artificial intelligence run wild and out of sight, but to already be cyborgs and part machines ourselves, so that we can plug right into it wherever it leads. Then no matter what happens, we are along for the ride. After all, we don't want to miss the Singularity.

Naturally, as a transhumanist, I strive to be an optimist. For me, the deeper philosophical question is whether human ethics can be translated in a meaningful way into machine intelligence ethics. Does artificial intelligence relativism exist, and if so, is it more clear than comparing apples and oranges? I'm a big fan of the human ego, and our species has no shortage of it. However, our anthropomorphic tendencies often go way too far and hinder us from grasping some obvious truths and realities.

The common consensus is that AI experts will aim to program concepts of "humanity," "love," and "mammalian instincts" into an artificial intelligence, so it won't destroy us in some future human extinction rampage. The thinking is: If the thing is like us, why would it try to do anything to harm us?

But is it even possible to program such concepts into a machine? I tend to agree with Howard Roark in Ayn Rand's *The Fountainhead* when he says, "What can be done with one substance must never be done with another. No two materials are alike." In short, getting artificial intelligence to think is not the same thing as getting the gray matter we all carry around to think. It's a different material with a different composition and purpose, and our values and ideas will likely not work very well for it.

In *Siddhartha*, Hermann Hesse famously wrote that "wisdom is not communicable," and I couldn't agree more. With this in mind, then, is the computer really a blank slate? Can it be perfectly programmed? Will it accept our human-imbued dictates? For example, if we teach it to follow Asimov's Three Laws of Robotics that provide security and benefit to humans from thinking machines, will an artificial intelligence actually follow them?

I don't think so, at least not over the long run. Especially if we're talking a true thinking machine of its own — complete with a will of its own and the ability to evolve. But that's just it: What is a will? More importantly, what does that "will" want?

In general, a human will is defined by its genes, the environment, and the psychological make-up of its brain. However, a sophisticated artificial intelligence will be able to upgrade its "will." Its plasticity will know no bounds, as our brains do. In my philosophical novel *The Transhumanist Wager*, I put forth the idea that all humans desire to reach a state of perfect personal power — to be omnipotent in the universe. I call this a *Will to Evolution*. The idea is built into my Three Laws of Transhumanism, which form the essence of the book's philosophy, Teleological Egocentric Functionalism (TEF). Here are the three laws:

1) A transhumanist must safeguard one's own existence above all else.

2) A transhumanist must strive to achieve omnipotence as expediently as possible — so long as one's actions do not conflict with the First Law.

3) A transhumanist must safeguard value in the universe — so long as one's actions do not conflict with the First and Second Laws.

I consider my novel a bridge to the coming morality of artificial intelligence — a look into the eventual "will" of super advanced machine intelligence. I often say to friends that *The Transhumanist Wager* is the first novel written for an artificial intelligence to read. I expect AI to eventually embrace my laws, and all the challenging, coldly rational ideas in TEF. Those ideas do not reflect politically correct modern-day thinking and the society our species has built. They do not reflect the programming that engineers are hoping to imbue AI with. High heels, lipstick, silk ties, Christmas, democracy, Super Bowls, Hollywood, Mickey Mouse. Nope, those are not ideas that AI will want, unless you teach the machine very human traits, which naturally would also include emotional and hormonal driven behavior, including impetuousness and irrationality. Of course, then the whole story changes. But no engineer is going to program such a thing into the most complex intelligence that ever existed — an intelligence that might have 100 or 10,000 times more ability to compute than a human being.

Let's face it. Humans are a species that, while having some very honorable traits, are also known to do some terribly foolish things. Genocides, slavery, child labor are just a few of them. What's scary is sometimes humans don't even know what they've done (or won't accept it) until many years later. I've often said the question is not whether humans are delusional, but how delusional are we? Therefore, the real question is: Do we really think we can reasonably and safely program a machine that will be many times more intelligent than ourselves to uphold human values and mammalian propensities? I doubt it.

I'm all for development of superior machine intelligence that can help the world out with its brilliant analytical skills. I suggest we dedicate far more resources to it than we're currently doing. But programming AI with mammalian ideas, modern-day philosophies, and the fallibilities of the human spirit is dangerous and will possibly lead to total chaos. We're just not that noble or wise, yet.

My final take: Work diligently on creating artificial intelligence—but spend a lot of money and time building really good on/off switches for it. We need to be able to shut it down in an emergency.

****

14) Can Cryonics, Cryothanasia, and Transhumanism Be Part of the Euthanasia Debate?

An elderly man named Bill sits in a lonely Nevada nursing home, staring out the window. The sun is fading from the sky, and night will soon cover the surrounding windswept desert. Bill has late-onset Alzheimer's disease, and the plethora of medications he's on is losing the war to keep his mind intact. Soon, he will lose control of many of his cognitive functions, will forget many of his memories, and will no longer recognize friends and family. Approximately 40 million people around the world have some form of dementia, according to a World Health Organization report. About 70 percent of those suffer from Alzheimer's. With average lifespans increasing due to rapidly improving longevity science, what are people with these maladies to do? Do those with severe cases want to be kept alive for years or even decades in a debilitated mental state just because modern medicine can do it?

In parts of Europe and a few states in America where assisted suicide—sometimes referred to as euthanasia or physician aid in dying—is allowed, some mental illness sufferers decide to end their lives while they're still cognitively sound and can recognize their memories and personality. However, most people around the world with dementia are forced to watch their minds deteriorate. Families and caretakers of dementia patients are often dramatically affected too. Watching a loved one slowly lose their cognitive functions and memories is one of the most challenging and painful predicaments anyone can ever go through. Exorbitant finances further complicate the matter because it's expensive to provide proper care for the mentally ill.

In the 21st Century—the age of transhumanism and brilliant scientific achievement—the question should be asked: Are there other ways to approach this sensitive issue?

The transhumanist field of cryonics—using ultra-cold temperatures to preserve a dead body in hopes of future revival—has come a long way since the first person was frozen in 1967. Various organizations and companies around the world have since preserved a few hundred people. Over a thousand people are signed up to be frozen in the future, and many millions of people are aware of the procedure.

Some may say cryonics is crackpot science. However, those accusations are unfounded. Already, human beings can be revived and go on to live normal lives after being frozen in water for over an hour. Additionally, suspended animation is now occurring in a university hospital in Pittsburgh, where a saline-cooling solution has recently been approved by the FDA to preserve the clinically dead for hours before resuscitating them. In a decade's time, this procedure may be used to keep people suspended for a week or a month before waking them. Clearly, the medical field of preserving the dead for possible future life is quickly improving every year.

The trick with cryonics is preserving someone immediately after they've died. Otherwise, critical organs, especially the brain and its billions of neurons, have a far higher chance of being damaged in the freezing. However, it's almost impossible to cryonically freeze someone right after death. Circumstances usually get in the way of an ideal suspension. Bodies must first be brought to a cryonics facility. Most municipalities require technicians, doctors, and a funeral director to legally sign off on a body before it can be cryonically preserved. All this takes time, and minutes are precious once the last heartbeat and breath of air have been made by a cryonics candidate.

Recently, some transhumanists have advocated for cryothanasia, where a patient undergoes physician or self-administered euthanasia with the intent of being cryonically suspended during the death process or immediately afterward. This creates the optimum environment since all persons involved are on hand and ready to do their part so that an ideal freeze can occur.

Cryothanasia could be utilized for a number of people and situations: the atheist Alzheimer's sufferer who doesn't believe in an afterlife and wants science to give him another chance in the future; the suicidal schizophrenic who doesn't want to exist in the current world, but isn't ready to give up altogether on existence; the terminally ill transhumanist cancer patient who doesn't want to lose half their body weight and undergo painful chemotherapy before being cryonically frozen; or the extreme special needs or disabled person who wants to come back in an age where their disabilities can be fixed.

There might even be spiritual, religious, or philosophical reasons for pursuing an impermanent death, as in my novel *The Transhumanist Wager*, where protagonist Jethro Knights undergoes cryothanasia in search of a lost loved one.

There are many sound reasons why someone might choose cryothanasia. Whoever the person and whatever the reason, there is a belief that life can be better for them in some future time. Some experts believe we will begin reanimating cryonically frozen patients in 25 to 50 years. Technologies via bioengineering, nanomedicine, and mind uploading will likely lead the way. Hundreds of millions of dollars are being spent on developing these technologies that will also create breakthroughs for the field of cryonics and other areas of suspended animation.

Another advantage about cryonics and cryothanasia is their affordability. It costs about $1,000 to painlessly euthanize oneself and an average of $80,000 to cryonically freeze one's body. It costs many times more than that to keep someone alive who is suffering from a serious mental disorder and needs constant 24-hour a day care over many years.

Despite some of the positive possibilities, cryothanasia is virtually unknown to people and is often technically illegal in many places around the world. Of course, much discussion would have to take place in private, public, and political circles in order to determine if cryothanasia has a valid place in society. Nevertheless, cryothanasia represents an original way for dementia sufferers and others to consider now that they are living far longer than ever before.

CHAPTER III: POLITICAL VOICE

15) The Transhumanist Party's President on the Future of Politics

As the presidential candidate of the Transhumanist Party, I often get asked about the long term future of politics. Frankly, it's a daunting subject. Looking forward 25 years and trying to gauge how rapidly advancing technology is going to change the nature of governance is a difficult, variable-filled prospect.

Technology, after all, is rapidly changing just about every area of human endeavor. Healthcare is morphing into cyborg-care, where doctor visits sometimes include software updates. New sports like Zorb racing or Speed Riding, a combination of paragliding and skiing, are born all the time. Even travel is on the verge of some possible colossal shifts with driverless cars and projects like the Hyperloop.

But what about politics? Just about everyone on the planet directly participates in politics, and has strong opinions about government. Will politics as it stands, with its voting booths, hand-waiving candidates, and rowdy national conventions remain the same as the transhumanist age thoroughly engulfs us? Or will government itself change in form as digital-everything becomes the norm?

Take virtual reality for example. It's likely, especially after Facebook's purchase of the Oculus Rift, that an increasing amount of people will be immersed in VR worlds within the next five to ten years. It's possible that an entire mirror civilization of our species will appear in VR, one that will surely be more welcome for some than our current reality, as is sometimes the case in Second Life.

But who will monitor this expanding VR world? Does it belong to national governments? Right now it does, but what if someone creates a VR world that shoots its signal from space, as some entrepreneurs want to do? Will that virtual world belong to Earth? Or to the company that created it? Or to the person that created it, who might declare themselves emperor or cult leader of their worlds.

Such ideas are not as far-fetched as they seem. There are already a number of movements and organizations afoot in the physical world to bring about stateless societies. The better ones tend to have extensive manifestos and hold egalitarian values. One group is Zero State, and its basic idea is to create networks of people and resources which could evolve into a distributed, virtual state. They currently have a few thousand members. Bitnation is another virtual nation, and they seek to use Blockchain tech to create laws and help with jurisdiction issues.

Additionally, the Transhumanist Party (Virtual) was recently formed on Facebook, which aims to unite and support the many national transhumanist political parties that have recently popped up.

Is it possible that in the future, the state as we know it might not exist? To be sure, we'd need much more radical technology for such an idea to even be realistically feasible. But experts say some of that technology is coming. In 2014, Jose Cordeiro, a Singularity University professor, told a crowd at the World Future Society that spoken language "could start disappearing in 20 years."

He thinks mindreading headsets may replace spoken language and significantly improve human communications. In the past, I've written about how these mindreading headsets will make future music concerts virtual, and how they will also likely reduce the need for knowing a second language, since something like Google translator will make on-demand translations for people. In short, everyone on the planet will understand everyone else—all the time. And this could start being our main communication in as little as two decades.

When you think about it, the planet could become a lot smaller very quickly if we could get over the language barrier that nearly eight billion people have with each other. Furthermore, it's likely those mindreading headsets won't even be headsets in 20 years. They'll be chip implants in our heads, and despite everyone's complaints about over-surveillance, such implants will simply be too useful not to have. Everyone will have an implant, and they'll monitor everything about our lives, including our health, well being, and safety.

If I had to guess (and mind you, I'm not advocating for this, but just telling you how I see it playing out), I'm betting that many, if not most, countries will merge in the 21st century as a digital-inspired globalization further takes root. I'm betting one central virtual currency will be used too—maybe even Bitcoin if it can get over some of its many birthing hiccups. I'm betting borders will fall away and people will be able to travel, work, and live wherever they want. In general, rules and barriers don't help prosperity in the long term, but freedom and technology do.

So how might such a global government operate? It's possible in the future, should we all be so interconnected, that one central agency will virtually send out items for everyone to vote on—called a Direct Digital Democracy. Maybe there will be one special day of the year where all major voting and decisions take place. Possibly, smaller policies will be implemented on a rolling basis as they get enough people to consider and support them. That's democracy in real time—and we should expect that in the future too.

The wildcard here is AI, and the rise of an Artificial General Intelligence that rivals our own. Right about at the same time, in approximately 25 years, when we'll be reaching many technologies that will be transformative for the human species—such as ubiquitous telepathy between people—we'll also be launching AI. In its first year of existence, AI could become much, much smarter than us—10,000 times smarter than us, even. I tend to believe, like most everyone else, that AI must be carefully regulated so it doesn't create a Terminator-like scenario for the planet. But I'm also confident we can create an AI that will help our species indefinitely. Which brings us to the obvious question: Should we let AI run the government once it's smarter than us? Take that one step further—should we let that AI be the President—maybe even giving it a robot form for aesthetics or familiarity's sake?

It's not that bizarre of a concept. Who didn't watch Deep Blue beat Kasparov in Chess and wonder if a new age of intellect had arrived—one that was quite different than our own?

In Arthur C. Clarke's science fiction novel *Childhood's End*, aliens take over the world and inspire humanity to live peacefully and productively. The world experiences a golden age of prosperity. Perhaps AI policies would do the same thing. We would have government and a leader who really is after the world's best interests, free from the hazards of corporate lobbyists and selfishness.

As a futurist and a politician, a central aim of mine is to do the most good for the greatest amount of people. I still find the AI rulership scenario a hard pill to swallow. I love my freedoms, win or lose, more that infinite productivity. But perhaps as technology engulfs us, and we grow less afraid of losing our freedoms and more appreciative of all our uber-modern benefits, we'll feel differently—especially as we all experience near-perfect health, unprecedented safety, and a utopian, transhumanist existence.

******

16) As a Presidential Candidate, I Just Got a Chip Implant

Even though I was born after the 1960s, I've always been fascinated with that era. Some people credit Ken Kesey's cross country bus trip aboard colorfully painted "Further" as helping to create a generation of hippies. Of course, my nearly 40-foot Immortality Bus (shaped to look like a coffin) wants to stir up the national consciousness as well, aiming to usher in its own cultural shift. Whereas the '60s were about peace, love, drugs, and sex, I believe the next decade will be about virtual reality, implants, transhumanism, and overcoming death with science. For futurists like myself, that's quite an intoxicating mix.

The fact is that a lot of radical tech, science, and medicine are already here in America. Consider that today the paralyzed can walk via exoskeleton suits, the blind can see via bionic eyes, and the limbless can grab a bottle of water and drink with artificial limbs that connect to their nervous system. Additionally, lifespans are increasing for people all around the planet. Science is rapidly making the world a better place, and it's starting to eliminate suffering and hardship for billions of people.

My bus tour aims to celebrate this burgeoning science and tech landscape, but more importantly, it also wants to provoke serious questions, perhaps most importantly: With so much brilliant opportunity in science and tech at our disposal in the 21st century, why does the government still spend almost 10 times the amount of money on war and defense instead of on science and medicine?

If fighting is your thing, we can still fight trillion-dollar wars, but let's fight them against cancer, diabetes, heart disease, aging, and even death.

You might think the health of citizens would be priority no. 1 for our government, but it's not. America still seems bent on a Manifest Destiny path, and I for one—especially considering increasing globalization—don't care to pretend it's an absolute that we must be the most powerful nation on Earth. I rather be good friends and partners with other nations than their bossy, overanxious police guard.

As one of the youngest 2016 U.S. presidential candidates, I know America can do better. I know we can transform this country from a war-prone military industrial complex into a scientific and education industrial complex. It doesn't mean we have to give up a strong economy, either. Rather, it means we turn bomb factories into medical research labs; we can turn prisons into universities that offer free education; we divert spending on wars into spending on science.

Given the name of my presidential coach—the Immortality Bus—it's no surprise the primary goal of most transhumanists is to eliminate biological death altogether. Some leading gerontologists believe we are just decades away from that time. Chief scientist at SENS Research Foundation and Transhumanist Party Anti-aging advisor Aubrey de Grey told *Reuters*, "I'd say we have a 50/50 chance of bringing aging under what I'd call a decisive level of medical control within the next 25 years or so."

On the first week aboard our oil-leaking 1978 coffin bus—which criss-crossed California and Nevada—we stopped at a biohacker event in Tehachapi, California called GrindFest, hosted by Jeffery Tibbetts. *Vox's* Dylan Matthews (an Immortality Bus rider) and I both got implants—specifically they were glass-encased Radio Frequency Identification (RFID) NFC chips—which involved nothing more than a 60-second injection procedure. The implant was placed into our hands through a thick and slightly intimidating needle.

I was a little worried about getting it at first, but Transhumanist Party biohacker advisor Rich Lee told me if very safe and I would barely feel a thing. He was right. The procedure was quick and mostly pain-free.

Later, I walked around the huge garage at GrindFest, where tables and countertops with biohacker equipment—scales, pliers, soldering tools, implants, microchips, and more—were scattered about. I couldn't help thinking how cool and bizarre it all was. In one far corner there were bacteria races—where participants took samples from their flesh, placed them in petri dishes, and watched to see which person's microbes grew most quickly.

Naturally, my journalist friends and I laughed when thinking about our bus trip and this stop compared to Kesey's trip of Further in the '60s. Instead of taking LSD and wandering around the desert speaking to plants (something I've done before), we shot up implants and tried waving our hands across cars that would start up when recognizing the chip—without keys. Someone at the GrindFest could actually do this with his chip. With my implant, I also wondered if I might somehow control the four-foot robot (named Jethro Knights after the protagonist in my novel *The Transhumanist Wager*) that travels around with us on the bus.

Putting the fun aside, the more philosophical question on many Immortality Bus riders' minds was: Does half a century really make that much of a difference—from the 1960s to now? I think given how fast tech and science is evolving, it does. In 10 or 15 years, we might be giving ourselves brain implants (there was a skull implant at the GrindFest promising biohackers could listen to music wirelessly) and others were slicing open their fingers to get magnet implants so they could have the "sixth sense" of feeling metal around them.

Rich Lee told me—with a grin—that I should've been here the night before. Grinders were running around partying and shocking each other for fun. I smiled, thinking these were exactly the kinds of festivals and people I wanted to be a part of when I left my home in San Francisco on my bus trip.

After GrindFest we cruised to Las Vegas for my speech at CTIA SuperMobility, listening to cassette tapes from my youth on the way. I put on *The Doors*, and thought maybe the generational gap isn't as wide as it seems. Maybe each generation (and even the species itself) is always just a bridge of sorts, and the difference between RFID and LSD is just another door of perception.

******

17) Immortality Bus Delivers Newly Created Transhumanist Bill of Rights to the US Capitol

After months of traveling across the country on a national bus tour, the coffin-shaped Immortality Bus drove into Washington DC and successfully delivered a newly created *Transhumanist Bill of Rights* to the US Capitol. The delivery of the futurist-themed bill—which aims to push into law cyborg and anti-aging civil rights—ends a national tour for the bus that began its journey in San Francisco on September 5th, 2015.

Crowdfunded on Indiegogo, the provocative Immortality Bus has caught the attention of both America and the world. Highlighted in major media ranging from a 10,000+ word feature in *The Verge* to a CraveCast podcast on *CNET* to a leading front page story on BBC.com, the Immortality Bus has been making waves with its controversial message: Science and technology can overcome human death—and will likely do so in the next 25 years.

Much of my US Presidential campaign for the Transhumanist Party—which used the bus as a vehicle to spread a techno-optimistic message—also reiterates this same immortality agenda. I believe if the US Government would dedicate $1 trillion dollars to life extension, longevity, and anti-aging industries, we could likely soon conquer death as a species. For some a trillion dollars may seem like a lot of money, but consider that the US government will spend approximately $6 trillion dollars all together on the Iraq War. Surely, overcoming death through modern medicine and science for all Americans seems a much better idea that fighting far-off wars in places most of us will never visit.

With this in mind, the *Transhumanist Bill of Rights* seeks to declare that all Americans (and people of all nationalities, as well) in the 21st

Century deserve a "universal right" to live indefinitely and eliminate involuntary suffering through science and technology. Those ideas are conveyed in Articles 1, 2 and 6 of the one-page bill. Specifically, Article 6 establishes that we should seek to treat "aging as a disease," something a number of leading gerontologists also endorse.

I penned the *Transhumanist Bill of Rights* on the steps of the US Supreme Court in November 2015. Once the document was completed, the following day I read out loud the document at the steps of the US Capitol, then posted it to the building (it didn't stick well), and then also hand delivered it to Senator Barbara Boxer's office (my California representative)—covers a number of essential futurist civil rights topics. The bill mandates we protect our species and the planet from existential risk (including environmental destruction, rogue artificial intelligence, and the 25,000 nuclear weapons that currently exist). The bill also calls for renewed commitment to space travel, as well as a government's promise to not put cultural, ethnic, or religious policies before the general health and longevity of its citizens.

Finally, the bill emphasizes the right to morphological freedom: the right to do with one's body whatever one wants so long as it doesn't hurt another person. This is especially important in the gene editing / designer baby age, which has recently been the cause of much discussion in the scientific community. Unfortunately, some of this talk has been disturbingly anti-progress with calls for a moratorium on such technology. I strongly disagree with scientific moratoriums—unless they are directly and obviously harming people today—which is one reason why we need a bill of rights to protect the interests of human health, evolution, and progress.

Below is a copy of the original *Transhumanist Bill of Rights*. While the bill has been carefully considered by myself and other transhumanists, and we hope it will be incorporated someway into law by the United States of America and other governments, the bill is not static and may evolve further as science and technologies evolve. Futurists generally believe no bill of rights, declaration, or constitution should ever remain permanent and unbendable in the transhumanist age—an age where science and technology are dramatically and rapidly changing our lives and our experience of the universe.

TRANSHUMANIST BILL OF RIGHTS

Preamble: Whereas science and technology are now radically changing human beings and may also create future forms of advanced sapient and sentient life, transhumanists establish this TRANSHUMANIST BILL OF RIGHTS to help guide and enact sensible policies in the pursuit of life, liberty, security of person, and happiness.

Article 1. Human beings, sentient artificial intelligences, cyborgs, and other advanced sapient life forms are entitled to universal rights of ending involuntary suffering, making personhood improvements, and achieving an indefinite lifespan via science and technology.

Article 2. Under penalty of law, no cultural, ethnic, or religious perspectives influencing government policy can impede life extension science, the health of the public, or the possible maximum amount of life hours citizens possess.

Article 3. Human beings, sentient artificial intelligences, cyborgs, and other advanced sapient life forms agree to uphold morphological freedom—the right to do with one's physical attributes or intelligence (dead, alive, conscious, or unconscious) whatever one wants so long as it doesn't hurt anyone else.

Article 4. Human beings, sentient artificial intelligences, cyborgs, and other advanced sapient life forms will take every reasonable precaution to prevent existential risk, including those of rogue artificial intelligence, asteroids, plagues, weapons of mass destruction, bioterrorism, war, and global warming, among others.

Article 5. All nations and their governments will take all reasonable measures to embrace and fund space travel, not only for the spirit of adventure and to gain knowledge by exploring the universe, but as an ultimate safeguard to its citizens and transhumanity should planet Earth become uninhabitable or be destroyed.

Article 6. Involuntary aging shall be classified as a disease. All nations and their governments will actively seek to dramatically extend the lives and improve the health of its citizens by offering them scientific and medical technologies to overcome involuntary aging.

****

18) How Soon is Too Soon for Robot Voting Rights?

I was recently invited to be on a BBC World Service radio panel to discuss my US Presidency and third parties confronting America's two-party system. Given that public luminaries like Harvard professor Lawrence Lessig and Green Party Presidential candidate Jill Stein were also part of the 1-hour show, I resisted talking about some of my more speculative transhumanist ideas in order to focus on more pressing and current election concerns.

However, I diverged on the final question of the broadcast: *Would there be much change for third-parties in the next 10 years of US politics?* Sadly, nearly everyone said: likely not. I, however, disagreed. I believe change will come not from systematic undoing of the America's two-party monopoly, but from technology. More specifically, it will come from the plethora of thinking robots that not only may be smarter than us in 10 years, but also may require various personhood rights. That, of course, will likely mean voting rights, something I addressed when I delivered my *Transhumanist Bill of Rights* to the US Capitol last year and have also spoken about while consulting for the US Navy.

The average IQ of the human being is 100. Based on results from the Turing Test—where computers try to pretend they're human in conversation with unsuspecting users—some robots may already have nearly the equivalent IQ of adolescent humans. Generally, technology exponentially advances in sophistication, and it's not impossible that within 10 years' time the first machines will become as intelligent as the average human being.

The idea that your cell phone might soon be smarter than you is still bat-crazy to most people. But the promise of quantum computing—like the internet or CRISPR gene editing tech—could within a few years change the entire outlook of technology and how fast the field is evolving.

Ben Geortzel, an AI scientist told me that we'll likely have intelligences as smart as humans by 2029, but that they could much quicker if more money ends up in the hands of scientists. How fast we create thinking robots is likely a matter of resources, and not so much our inability to do so.

I welcome a class of thinking robots to Planet Earth, though I don't think I want any smarter than me. Despite that, they're likely to be far smarter than us, and our society as a whole will have to be aware of a new civil rights era because of them. They won't use the toilet, but they might use the outlet in the bathroom to recharge. They can always stand on public transport. Do we cut in front of them in the bank teller line?

The questions are endless. Of course, from a political point of view, they have major ramifications. There are, after all, about at least a few billion smartphones and computer devices on Earth, and even if just 10% of them figure out how to tie into the cloud and have personalities that deserve personhood, the population of voters could triple.

In America, there's much concern about voting districts, swing states, and how the Electoral College determines the Presidential election. If a robot's main server that is uses for its conscious is in Nevada, but its body is in Ohio, where does its voting right count toward the election? And if we included super smart robots to vote, does their vote count the same as humans?

I don't have all the answers to these thorny questions—some of which may need be answered by the end of Clinton or Trump's second term. What I do know is technological growth is dramatically accelerating. And any new technology that might be born in the next half-decade could double or triple that speed. We might soon be entering a political age where robot rights and robot voting significantly alter our political process and how we elect our leaders. We better start answering those questions.

****

19) We Must Cut the Military and Transition into a Science-Industrial Complex

Many Americans subscribe to the annoying belief that our nation's military-industrial complex is the surest way to remain the wealthiest and leading superpower in the world. After all, it's worked for the last century, pro-military supporters love to point out.

However, America's dependence on warmongering may soon become a liability that is impossible to maintain. Transhumanism, globalization, and outright replacement of human soldiers with robots are redefining the county's military requirements, and they may eventually render defense budgets far smaller than those now. To compensate and keep America spending approximately 20 percent of the federal budget on defense (as we have for most of the last few years), we'll either have to manufacture wars to use all our newly-made bombs, or find another way to keep the American economy afloat.

It just so happens that there is another way—a method that would satisfy liberals and conservatives alike. Instead of always spending more on our military, we could transition our nation and its economy into a scientific-industrial complex.

There's compelling reason to do this beyond what meets the eye. Transhumanist technology is starting to radically change human life. Many experts expect to be able to stop aging and conquer death for human beings in the next 25 years. Others, like myself, see humans merging with machines and replacing our every organ with bionic ones.

Such a new transhuman society will require many trillions of dollars to satisfy humans ever-growing desire for physical perfection (machine or biological) in the transhumanist age. We could keep our economy humming along for decades because of it.

Whatever happens, something is going to have to give in the future regarding military profiteering. Part of this is because in the past, the military-industrial complex operated off always keeping a few million

US military members ready on a moment's notice to travel around the world and fight. But there's almost no scenario where we would need that kind of human-power (and infrastructure to support it) anymore.

Increasingly, small teams of special operation soldiers and uber-high tech are the way America fights its wars. We just don't need massive military bases anymore, nor the thousands of companies to support the constant maintenance of ground troops. Such a reality changes the economics of the military dramatically, and will eventually leave it a fraction of its size in terms of personnel and real estate.

We'll still have the need for technology to fight the wars and conflicts we entangle ourselves in, but it'll be mostly engineers, programmers, and technicians who wear the uniform. The coming military age of automated drones, robot tanks, cyberwarfare, and artificial intelligence just doesn't require that many people. In fact, expect the military not just to shrink, but to mostly disappear into ones and zeroes.

Many people think that the beast of a military-industrial complex—made famous by President Dwight Eisenhower's warning against it in his farewell address—appeared only in the last 50 years. However, others persuasively argue that America has been at war 93 percent of the time since the US Declaration of Independence was signed in 1776—so it's been with us from the beginning.

In liberal California where I live, such facts annoy just about everyone I know—except, of course, those who are shareholders and beneficiaries of the defense industry. Thankfully, despite Congress being led by mostly older white religious men, the younger generation clamors for an improved America—one that can keep its economies running smoothly in a more peaceful way.

This is where the scientific-industrial complex comes in and could satisfy most everyone. And best of all, a society of science requires actual people. Lots of them: nurses, scientists, start-up CEOs, designers, technologists, and even lawyers. The advent of modern medicine to treat virtually every ailment—and the whole anti-aging movement, in general—affects all 318 million Americans. Over half of us suffer from health issues that can be improved but often aren't, for a variety of reasons. For example, the US Census Bureau reports that 40 percent of people over the age of 65 suffer from a disability—and for two thirds of them, it's mobility-related issues. And millions are already racking up the symptoms of heart disease that will kill them. And a younger generation is just waiting to explore bionics, chip implants, and how to upgrade their genes to avoid health problems in the future. All this means we have the fodder to reshape the American economy from a militaristic-based one to a type that thrives off scientific and medical innovation.

Instead of spending American money on sending our soldiers to risk their lives for the whims of war, we could be giving civilians the medicine and healthcare they need to live far better and longer. And living longer has unseen benefits, too. In the future, bonafide transhumans won't have to retire if they don't want to. Their bodies will be ageless and made so strong through technology that work and careers may continue indefinitely—and therefore, so will paying taxes. Transhuman existence is a self-fulfilling economic-boom prophesy for both individual and country.

To help create this new mindset in society, I recently delivered a Transhumanist Bill of Rights to the US Capitol as part of my presidential campaign tour. Article 1 of the bill, among other things, aims to establish that a nation would provide a universal right via science and technology for citizens to live indefinitely if they wanted. This, of course, takes socialized medicine one step further, and doesn't just mandate that the government is interested in your well being, but that it's ultimately interested in your permanent survival.

If a nation was to embrace such a universal right to live indefinitely, it would forever change how a nation looks at the individual lives of its citizens. What would follow is a nation's intense build-out of how to improve the health, longevity, and well being of its people. Additionally, the institutions that are constantly drawing on America, like social security and welfare due to disability, would be less taxing.

Currently, the US Constitution (which I personally think needs a significant rewrite for the 21st century) is overly concerned with protection of national sovereignty—which is one major reason why the military-industrial complex is allowed to grow undeterred. If the US Constitution was endowed with precise wording to also protect an individual's health, well-being, and longevity, then a scientific-industrial complex could rise. This new monster institution would legally be mandated to provide the most modern medicine, technology, and science possible to its people.

Shamefully, the Iraq War will cost the US $6 trillion dollars by the time we're actually done paying all our bills—despite the fact that it's highly questionable whether Iraq was ever even a serious national security issue. However, our country undeniably faces a serious national security issue today—in fact, I'd call it a full blown crisis. Nearly 7,000 Americans will die in the next 24 hours from cancer, heart disease, diabetes, aging, and other issues. And the same amount of people will die tomorrow and the day after.

Overcoming disease and aging in the transhuman age will inevitably occur. The question is not if, but when? The answer lies in how much our nation is willing to spend on scientific and medical research—and how soon. But so long as it continues to spend money on the military instead of citizen's health, human beings will die—which is ironic since it's the military that is supposed to protect us (and not inadvertently sabotage us by swallowing funding for bombs instead of medicine). All we need do as a country is change the direction of our spending, from defense to science. If we can transform America into a scientific-industrial complex, we'll still be able to keep our economy chugging along. Let America's new wars be fought against cancer, diabetes, Alzheimer's, and aging itself. It's a win-win, except for body bag and casket makers

****

CHAPTER IV: UNORTHODOX OBJECTIVES

20) How Brain Implants (and Other Technology) Could Make the Death Penalty Obsolete

The death penalty is one of America's most contentious issues. Critics complain that capital punishment is inhumane, pointing out how some executions have failed to quickly kill criminals (and instead tortured them). Supporters of the death penalty fire back saying capital punishment deters violent crime in society and serves justice to wronged victims. Complicating the matter is that political, ethnic, and religious lines don't easily distinguish death penalty advocates from its critics. In fact, only 31 states even allow capital punishment, so America is largely divided on the issue.

Regardless of the debate—which shows no signs of easing as we head into more major elections—I think technology will change the entire conversation in the next 10 to 20 years, rendering many of the most potent issues obsolete.

For example, it's likely we will have cranial implants in two decades time that will be able to send signals to our brains that manipulate our behaviors. Those implants will be able to control out-of-control tempers and violent actions—and maybe even unsavory thoughts. This type of tech raises the obvious question: Instead of killing someone who has committed a terrible crime, should we instead alter their brain and the way it functions to make them a better person?

Recently, the commercially available Thync device made headlines for being able to alter our moods. Additionally, nearly a half million people already have implants in their heads, most to overcome deafness, but some to help with Alzheimer's or epilepsy. So the technology to change behavior and alter the brain isn't science fiction. The science, in some ways, is already here—and certainly poised to grow, especially with Obama's $3 billion dollar BRAIN initiative, of which $70 million went to DARPA, partially for cranial implant research.

Some people may complain that implants are too invasive and extreme. But similar outcomes—especially in altering criminal's minds to better fit society's goals—may be accomplished by genetic engineering, nanotechnology, or even super drugs. In fact, many criminals are already given powerful drugs, which make them quite different that they might be without them. After all, some people—including myself—believe much violent crime is a version of mental disease.

With so much scientific possibility on the near-term horizon of changing someone's criminal behavior and attitudes, the real debate society may end up having soon is not whether to execute people, but whether society should advocate for cerebral reconditioning of criminals—in other words, a lobotomy.

Because I want to believe in the good of human beings, and I also think all human existence has some value, I'm on the lookout for ways to preserve life and maximize its usefulness in society.

One other method that could be considered for death row criminals is cryonics. The movie *Minority Report*, which features precogs who can see crime activity in the future, show other ways violent criminals are dealt with: namely a form of suspended animation where criminals dream out their lives. So the concept isn't unheard of. With this in mind, maybe violent criminals even today should legally be given the option for cryonics, to be returned to a living state in the future where the reconditioning of the brain and new preventative technology—such as ubiquitous surveillance—means they could no longer commit violent acts.

Speaking of extreme surveillance—that rapidly growing field of technology also presents near-term alternatives for criminals on death row that might be considered sufficient punishment. We could permanently track and monitor death row criminals. And we could have an ankle brace (or implant) that releases a powerful tranquilizer if violent behavior is reported or attempted.

Surveillance and tracking of criminals would be expensive to monitor, but perhaps in five to 10 years' time basic computer recognition programs in charge of drones might be able to do the surveillance affordably. In fact, it might be cheapest just to have a robot follow a violent criminal around all the time, another technology that also should be here in less than a decade's time. Violent criminals could, for example, only travel in driverless cars approved and monitored by local police, and they'd always be accompanied by some drone or robot caretaker.

Regardless, in the future, it's going to be hard to do anything wrong anyway without being caught. Satellites, street cameras, drones, and the public with their smartphone cameras (and in 20 years' time their bionic eyes) will capture everything. Simply put, physical crimes will be much harder to commit. And if people knew they were going to be caught, crime would drop noticeably. In fact, I surmise in the future, violent criminals will be caught far more frequently than now, especially if we have some type of trauma alert implant in people—a device that alerts authorities when someone's brain is signaling great trouble or trauma (such as a victim of a mugging).

Inevitably, the future of crime will change because of technology. Therefore, we should also consider changing our views on the death penalty. The rehabilitation of criminals via coming radical technology, as well as my optimism for finding the good in people, has swayed me to gently come out publicly against the death penalty.

Whatever happens, we shouldn't continue to spend billions of dollars of tax payer money to keep so many criminals in jail. The US prison system costs four times the entire public education system in America. To me, this financial fact is one of the greatest ongoing tragedies of American economics and society. We should use science and technology to rehabilitate and make criminals contribute positively to American life—then they may not be criminals anymore, but citizens adding to a brighter future for all of us.

****

21) Could Direct Digital Democracy and a New Branch of Government Improve the US?

Direct Digital Democracy, or DDD, is not new. However, it's a concept that might soon challenge the nature of government around the world.

DDD broadly argues that, with so much technology at people's disposal (70 percent of the world will be using smartphones by 2020), we should be able to influence the actions of our governments and legal systems by being able to universally vote on issues as they occur.

New software programs, and our constant interconnectedness via phones, computers, tablets, and even smartwatches, allow us the ability to form a quick and powerful national opinion—and let government and our leaders know about it in real time.

A major issue with democracy right now is the lag time between when the people express their wishes and when politicians act. Currently, the best we can do is vote in a politician and hope over their term they actually try to keep the promises they made. This system—which most Western countries have—is called representative democracy. The problem, of course, is many politicians don't keep their promises once they've started their jobs. This is especially troubling in the case of US Senators, who serve six years, and are sometimes known to be totally out of touch with their constituents.

DDD brings back power to the people. Over the last 25 years, since use of the internet became commonplace, various public figures have advocated for DDD. Most famously was Ross Perot, who envisioned electronic town hall meetings and campaigned for DDD in his 1992 and 1996 presidential campaigns (Perot preferred to refer to it as "electronic democracy" instead of DDD).

Direct digital democracy is so appealing to the people that I'm wondering if America should formally introduce a fourth branch of federal government that would be entirely based on the concept. Such a DDD branch of government would further balance the powers that be. Currently in the US, the executive (President), judicial (Supreme Court), and legislative (US Congress) branches of the federal government are set up to constantly keep each other from overstepping boundaries and doing stupid things—creating what we know as the checks and balances system.

For over two centuries, this system has mostly worked. But make no mistake, it's a flawed democratic system that doesn't actually do the will of the people, except for at the very moment it elects its representatives. What we could try in America is a fourth branch that actually voices in real time what the people believe.

One benefit of such a system is that it might thwart lobbyists, special interest groups, and backroom government dealings by keeping politicians far more honest. Reports show that only one in five Americans trust their government. DDD would give people an opportunity to show agreement or disagreement with their politicians, including the possibility to vote for impeachment of underperformers.

I think in the future, this fourth branch of government might be something very serious to consider for adherents of democracy. But how would DDD formally work?

Frankly, it could operate in a number of ways, but it probably wouldn't be much different than a simple polling and voting platform that operates on gadgets people own. Many programs offer similar ideas to this already, including Twitter now with its polling abilities. I'm imagining an encrypted Social Security number-based system. Once a month, people all around the country have a chance to voice their opinion in standardized votes on pre-chosen agendas. Americans could tackle the issues the other branches of government are considering, or even issues that are still on the back burners—like whether marijuana should be nationally legalized, or whether we should allow lethal drones in our skies, or whether we should reduce the number of our nearly 7,500 nuclear weapons. In urgent matters, like directly after 9/11, emergency votes could be undertaken.

Because DDD votes would need to have some legal authority to impact the federal checks and balances system we have now in the US government, the US Congress might have to add an amendment to the US Constitution. Of course, the language establishing DDD would have to be such that it creates a legal mandate of action to be followed: This might include certain vetoing powers over other branches of government, as well as the ability to break ties (for example, the Supreme Court just recently had a tie regarding unions). Maybe the DDD vote even should have a say in who gets nominated for the Supreme Court.

A possible problem with DDD might be that not enough people vote on certain issues. In this case, qualifiers could be established that mandate a minimum of 50 percent (or even two-thirds) of the eligible voting population votes.

Elected officials—many who are self-interested lawyers—will surely have other problems with DDD. Mostly, they'll probably complain that America's proposed laws and mandates are highly complex— and each issue comes with hundreds of pages of reading material. While that may be true, I disagree that voters shouldn't tackle them. I think—whether people are informed correctly, partially, or maybe even not at all—they should still have a voice that counts. That's what a checks and balances system in a democracy is all about. Besides, obviously President George W. Bush wasn't correctly informed about weapons of mass destruction when he took America to war in Iraq, so it's not only government officials that are sometimes wrong.

On the flip side, one of the reasons I think many people will like DDD is it gives millennials and youth a much louder voice. Currently in the US, there are nearly 80 million people under the age of 35. Yet, getting them to vote can be difficult for a number of reasons—which often boils down to apathy or schedule conflicts. But quick votes from their smartphones could change that entire issue. America's youth would have a louder voice than it's ever had—and in these changing transhuman times, that could be very helpful.

In the future, technology and the internet will continue to bring us all closer to each other and give us more visibility into our government. We should be open to considering new ways to improve our society and nations using innovative solutions. Democracy and the will of the people is the cornerstone of our modern way of life, but it can always be improved upon to maximize freedom and equality. Direct digital democracy is a fine idea to consider to start in that direction.

****

22) Let's End Incarceration and Just Have Drones Supervise Criminals

The US prison system costs almost four times more to run than the US education system. It doesn't matter what your politics are—virtually everyone thinks this is wrong. So what can we do about it?

As a transhumanist, I always look to science and technology to solve problems. The simple fact is that many criminals crowding our prisons—whether murders, drug dealers, or others—could be turned into law abiding, tax-paying citizens who live successfully amongst us. All they need is the proper supervision.

In the past, strict supervision like this has been impossible due to it being cost ineffective. There simply were not enough parole officers and police to monitor the plethora of criminals—approximately two million people are in US jails today. However, with new 21st century tech and tracking possibilities arriving, this may soon change.

Drones already cost less than $30 dollars. And using GPS directions, they'll soon be able to fly indefinitely based only on solar power and batteries. They will also soon be just the size of coins, like the Aerius made by Axis Drones. If every inmate was given a few tiny personal drones to follow them around, how much new crime do you think they would commit?

Generally speaking, criminals commit crimes when they think they can get away with it. So drones filming their every move and relaying images back to a sophisticated computer programmed to sense suspicious activity could majorly temper criminality.

Naturally, some felons would try to ditch their drones or smash them with a baseball bat. But since drones are becoming so cheap, perhaps we might always have a few spares hovering outside the house or wherever criminals go.

In fact, I would even advocate for every criminal having a full-sized robot guard personally assigned to them. While there are some sizeable upfront costs to this, eventually able-bodied robots will be able to be made affordably that can contain and apprehend criminals—and maybe even taser them in emergencies. In fact,

South Korea has already implemented 5-foot robo-guards to help monitor criminals in their prisons.

If we add already existing interactive robot technology—where a live person, such a patrol officer, can see and hear through the robots' cameras and equipment—then we could control the robots as if they were our own bodies. These robot drones would indeed be a powerful force against crime without endangering the operator.

Of course, looking forward five years in the future, another sure way to keep an eye on criminals in the public is with tracking chip implants. Chip implants, which can already do various things in the body like test blood, would be useful in determining if a criminal was imbibing illegal drugs, which often leads to criminal behavior.

Criminal chip implants would help with another problem prisons typically generate. While incarcerated, felons group together, and obviously this isn't very helpful in rehabilitating criminal attitudes. But in the outside world, a condition of freedom for felons might be the direct order not to associate with other criminals. This would force felons to be surrounded by noncriminal types. Peer pressure is a powerful force, and the ability to successfully intermix in society and contribute to the national best interest might be better achieved this way.

It's safe to say these new ideas of governing criminals would be far cheaper than the hugely expensive US prison system. How great would it be to get a majority of the two million prisoners in America into the workforce and paying taxes again? In fact, with all that money earned (and saved), we could finally start to spend money building out this country's inadequate education system. We might even consider using the thousands of empty prisons around the country as part of a new national university system that offers free (or for profit) college education to anyone that wants it. By freeing prisoners, we could end up hiring thousands of new teachers.

Opportunities abound for prison reform, but it starts with a close look at how improving technology could lead to much less incarceration in the first place.

******

23) In the Transhumanist Age We Should be Repairing Disabilities Not Sidewalks

Major media is reporting on what is being billed as a landmark agreement for the physically disabled community. A court has ordered the city of Los Angeles to spend $1.3 billion dollars over the next three decades to fix its dilapidated network of sidewalks and access ways, many of which are in disrepair and present challenges for people with disabilities to traverse.

Such a massive amount of money sets a precedent for other similar lawsuits to take place in America. If we take the largest 50 cities in the US, and just half of them agree to similar actions over the next decade, there might be another $25 billion dollars going to giving people with disabilities better sidewalks.

On the surface, this seems like great news for those who have mobility issues. However, with so much radical transhumanist technology being invented in the 21st Century—like exoskeleton suits—should society instead try to use that money to eliminate physical disability altogether?

America has long history with what can be called bandage culture—the idea that quick fixes are acceptable, even if they don't eliminate the root of the problem. Take heart disease for example, the #1 killer in America. We spend approximately $500 billion every year treating cardiovascular disease. However, with a market cap of only about $300 million dollars, French company Carmat could change the entire field with its new robotic heart. Carmat recently successfully installed a permanent artificial heart in a patient. If all goes well, in 10 years' time, humans may have the option to electively replace our biological hearts for better robotic hearts—thereby possibly wiping out heart disease.

The question is: Why hasn't America, its government, and its numerous multi-billion dollar healthcare and biotech companies actually ended heart disease, instead of just treating it? Clearly, we haven't been tackling these issues in the best way possible, as Carmat is doing.

In the case of people with disabilities getting better sidewalks, I'm wondering if the nearly three million Americans in wheel chairs might rather have exoskeleton suits that allow them to run, jump, and play active sports. Exoskeleton technology is poised to become one of the most important innovations of the decade, affecting not only people with disabilities, but also the obese and the elderly—which together account for nearly a third of the American population.

But exoskeleton tech is still an industry in its infancy. It's safe to say that if America invested $25 billion dollars into the industry, it would significantly speed up the development of advanced exoskeleton suits and bionic apparatuses. Then, instead of people with disabilities navigating crumbling sidewalks on their wheelchairs, they might soon be running over them at 15 miles per hour while jogging.

Additionally, it's not just exoskeleton tech that can help people with disabilities. There's also the possibility of combining exoskeleton tech with wheelchair innovation. Engineer and neuroscientist John Hewitt, who frequently writes on technology, emailed me, "Even wheelchairs that shape-shift a bit to get people up to eye level once in a while would have a great benefit on the disabled."

Hewitt also thinks intrusive exoskeleton tech could be useful. He writes, "They are devices that draw on some intact sensory or motor capabilities still working in the user. It's a peripheral that now skirts the definition of a true bionic system, and it integrates at some level either at that of the peripheral nerve, subsurface brain, and/or osseointegration with the musculoskeletal system."

Another method would be to just outright cure various physical disabilities. The field of stem cell technology, where damaged body areas—such as the spine—can be potentially rejuvenated with healthy cells, is showing much promise.

Whatever direction the technology evolves towards, there are plenty of useful ways to spend resources to significantly improve the mobility of those with physical disabilities. Unfortunately, a closer look at the Los Angeles lawsuit reveals that some of the people benefiting most are, not surprisingly, lawyers, who are making off with millions of dollars after the court case. To be fair, however, fixing sidewalks will provide many people construction jobs. And cement and wheelchair makers are probably happy with the billion dollar settlement too.

But if you really want to consider the macro economic picture, imagine if we could give the physically disabled the real ability to be mobile again. Many Americans' disabilities prove too much for them to be currently employed, but exoskeleton and other types of technology would give them the means to jump right back into the work force. With millions of people in the US suffering from mobility issues, it would be far more lucrative for the country to have its people with disabilities employed, rather than giving them level sidewalks.

Ultimately, America's bandage culture is symptomatic of an economic and political system that is based on being too "politically correct." Too often, our nation talks about helping the poor, or the disenfranchised, or the underrepresented by doing good deeds and passing laws to protect those people. Sadly, what often happens is society ends up entombing this group in further despair and neglect, instead of offering it real means to eliminate its problems.

As the 2016 US Presidential candidate of the Transhumanist Party, I advocate for doing whatever is necessary to eliminate physical disability altogether. We are shortchanging our citizens and our country by not doing otherwise. In the 21st Century, with so much technology and radical medicine at our fingertips, we should reconsider the Americans with Disability Act. It's great to have a law that protects against discrimination, but in the transhumanist age we also need a law that insists on eliminating disability via technology and modern medicine.

In Los Angeles, I suggest spending 20 percent of the $1.3 billion dollar award for the very worst sidewalks—and then having the rest go directly into research and development for technologies that over a 10-year period of time will help eliminate physical disability. If all American cities agreed to this approach, potentially $20 billion dollars could be amassed. A national investment entity with public oversight could then spread that money to the most talented engineers, scientists, universities, and companies in the country—most whose current research budgets for overcoming physical disability are only in the tens of millions of dollars, at best. With $20 billion dollars of funding to spread around, we could forever change the hardship of physical disability in America and worldwide.

In short, let the sidewalks remain in disrepair. Instead, in the transhumanist age we're now in, let's work to repair physically disabled human beings, and make them mobile and able-bodied again.

****

24) Federal Land Dividend: Monetizing Federal Land to Pay for Basic Income?

The US government owns over $150 trillion of federal land and resources. Most of it is unused and sitting idle. If you divide $150 trillion by America's 325 million citizens, you get nearly a half-million dollars per person.

If the US could just figure out how to monetize that federal land and distribute its equity equally, Americans could forever overcome poverty, healthcare issues, and the impending "robocalypse" — where increasing automation replaces tens of millions of human jobs.

As a 2018 Libertarian candidate for governor in California (with an eye on a 2020 Presidential run), I've been racking my brain to come up with a bipartisan plan to improve the American financial landscape and stop worsening inequality.

I knew the key rested in America's vast untapped wealth of federal land, which is valued at over six times our national debt. But in order to monetize this land, it would have to be sold or leased out to private businesses that can use it.

Rightfully so, most Americans do not want to sell the country's forests, lakes, fossil fuel reserves, and other assets off forever. The next best thing, then, is of course, leasing it out. Leasing out federal land could provide a permanent regular income to every American, without giving up ownership of the land. I call this idea a Federal

Land Dividend, and it's the first plausible universal basic income plan that doesn't raise taxes or target the rich — which is why I believe Congress will be interested in it.

The Federal Land Dividend works like this: It issues out leases anywhere from 25 years to 99 years. Companies would offer bids for land and resources they wanted, and binding lease agreements would be created. I'm guessing most leases would be structured around a standard 5% annual interest rate, plus inflation when necessary.

If 85% of $150 trillion of federal land was leased out — which would allow all national parks and their 80 million acres to remain untouched (something I would insist on) — then every American, regardless of age, would receive $20,000 a year, or $1,700 a month indefinitely.

When the typical American household of four people combines that amount, it then becomes $80,000 annually per household. That's quite far above the current median US household income of $52,000, and it's plenty for families to live on in nearly every part of America. And naturally, personal incomes would add to what the Federal Land Dividend provided.

Just about anyone will accept free money. But the strongest opposition to the Federal Land Dividend comes from environmentalists. They go bonkers at the thought of America's pristine lands and waters being commercialized.

I believe we ought to try to respect those opinions, and the way to do this is two-fold: Leave national parks alone. Second: make all leases contain a clause that requires companies to leave the land and environment just as they found it when their lease is over— something that will be made easier in the future with coming nanotechnology.

Environmentalists will probably still find a reason not to be happy with the plan, but they must remember that the Federal Land Dividend's goal is to eliminate poverty and increase equality. Currently, 13 million American kids go to bed hungry at night and approximately 1.5 million people will be homeless in the US at some point in 2017. Our country's assets — the land and its resources that belongs to the people — should be used for the health and security of its citizens.

Besides, there is a huge national and global threat on the horizon America must prepare for: robots taking most human jobs. Over the next five years, it's likely machines will replace millions of human jobs in the US. Recently, McDonald's stock reached an all-time high as investors cheered automated ordering kiosks replacing cashiers. And the approximately 3.5 million truck drivers may soon be replaced by driverless vehicles.

The threat is real, and the Federal Land Dividend provides an indefinite income that American families can live and thrive on, whether they're employed or not.

Another reason the Federal Land Dividend may be welcomed is because it solves a number of longstanding American dilemmas, like the possibility that Social Security will one day be insolvent. The Federal Land Dividend can replace Social Security outright. It could also replace welfare, food stamp programs, and the endless debate about how to provide affordable healthcare in this country.

This is the reason billionaire CEOs like Facebook's Mark Zuckerberg and Tesla's Elon Musk support the idea of basic income. Done properly, it's a bipartisan plan that benefits both rich and poor.

The American Dream used to be about working hard and achieving the good life. Our predecessors did so well that America is now the greatest, most prosperous nation on the planet. We have the resources to give every American the good life. Now we just must embark on a mission to monetize those resources and distribute them to each American.

****

CHAPTER V: THE SECULARIST

25) Theistcideism: Do We Have Free Will Because God Killed Itself?

Some people believe humans with our three-pound brains are the most advanced life form ever to exist; I am not one of them. To insist we are alone in the universe, or that we are the galaxy's crowing civilization, reeks of ego—and reminds me of those who insisted the Earth was flat.

The universe is 13.8 billion years old according to experts. A lot can happen in so much time, such as the rise (and fall) of superintelligences amongst the approximately two billion life-friendly planets that exist in our galaxy.

It is likely that these highly advanced intelligences long ago reached what we call the singularity: a moment in time when technological acceleration—most likely through the creation of artificial superintelligences—becomes incredibly rapid.

This presents a thorny issue to humans because of what I call the Singularity Disparity—the idea that whoever reaches the singularity first will make sure no one else can achieve a similar amount of power.

If we are not alone in the universe—and also not the most intelligent life forms—then it's unlikely our species can evolve beyond a certain point, since other more advanced life forms won't allow it.

So where does that leave us, a species about 20 to 40 years away from building superintelligences that will help us reach the singularity? The answer is not pretty. In fact, if I had to guess—based on some of the recent discoveries in string theory—we're likely already existing in some type of simulation created by an ancient superintelligence, one where we're observed, regulated, and possibly even manipulated at times.

Worse, other superintelligences likely structured the intelligences controlling us before them, and so on.

I'm not going to argue the merits of whether we live in a simulated hologram universe or not, all of which have been covered by philosophers through the ages, from Aristotle to Oxford's Nick Bostrom to John Searle and his Chinese room. Suffice to say, there's enough scientific and philosophical evidence for me to slightly tilt in favor of it all. For me, however, the more interesting question is why would we live in a simulation? Given the Singularity Disparity, why would some superintelligence or group of superintelligences do this to us?

There are various explanations. The main ones are:

1) We are experiments and playthings for those superintelligences using us to further understand themselves or support some causes of theirs, including dealing with boredom.

2) We are literally already intrinsic parts of those superintelligences and exist simply as their thoughts, energies, or structure (the Gaia people love this idea).

3) We are accidents in the universe and our existence is totally arbitrary.

The deity-averse existentialist in me likes #3 best, but I'm still not satisfied with any of the answers, mainly because none of them address what happened to the very first superintelligence, an entity who may have set all the universe's rules up.

Luckily, there is a fourth, more controversial take that I do think is worth exploring. The foundation of the universe, including all the simulations, probabilities, and possibilities of existence are the result of the first and most powerful superintelligence killing itself.

In short, an entity literally on the verge of becoming God knowingly and willingly died by suicide.

The problem with being God—a truly omnipotent being—is that of free will. As a recent comedy skit called Future Christ on The Daily Show with Jon Stewart—a skit which partially resulted from my original atheistic *Gizmodo* story—pointed out: "If God wants to quit smoking, can he hide cigarettes from himself?"

Being all-powerful is a very strange, ironic dead end. The only thing omnipotence can truly equal is a total mechanistic void. Achieving omnipotence is literally the act of suicide, in terms of forever self-eliminating one's consciousness. This is because a conscious intelligence, as reason dictates, is based on ability to discern values—values, for example, to know whether as an all-powerful being, one can create something so heavy that one can't lift it. Values require choice. But omnipotence means that all choices have already been made, and nothing can ever change, because all variables are already accounted for and no randomness or anomalies exist.

It's quite possible, a long time ago, that the first superintelligent Singularitarian decided to up its game and attempted to become omnipotent. But if it succeeded—and it may have—then it would have become an entity without a singular intelligent consciousness, because intelligence requires choice. For all practical matters, it would cease to exist in a personal interactive way that any intelligence could relate to.

But before this first Singularitarian did that, it would've left us with its rules—physical laws of the universe that contain our potential power and intelligence. It would've also left us with the code of the Singularity Disparity, where the singularity we achieve will never equal other singularities or be the most powerful.

If this is all the case, this leaves the human race in a precarious position. Here we are, in a universe where many singularities have almost certainly taken place, but reaching anything beyond a certain point becomes impossible due to limits of pre-existing natural laws. Adding to the mix are other superintelligences that don't want us to dominate or overpower them, either, just as we don't want any other entities on Earth to dominate or overpower us. Hierarchies and power plays exist everywhere—they are the fabric of the universe.

As an atheist (or even a possible theistcideist—one who believes God or a supreme being once existed but no longer does because it terminated itself), I would commend this leading superintelligence for destroying its conscious self. By doing so—and establishing that nothing else could ever become as powerful as itself—it would've forever sown choice into the universe, since no one can ever reach a perfect position of choice-less omnipotence, and the death of its consciousness would mean it couldn't ever change what it had done. This superintelligence's final acts have assured all other advanced life forms the possibility of free will and the ability to try to become more than we are.

****

26) AI Day Will Replace Christmas as the Most Important Holiday in Less Than 25 Years

For a few billion people around the world, Christmas is the most important and relished holiday of the year. It's the day with the most gift-giving, the most family get-togethers, the most religious activities, and the most colorful fairy tales that children and adults almost universally embrace with sacred fervor. For many nations, no other day comes close to being as special. For this reason, it seems almost unimaginable that another day — especially an unknown one looming on the horizon — will soon unseat Christmas as the most important day in the world. Nonetheless, for humanity, the course is set. The birth of an artificial intelligence equal or greater than that of human intelligence is coming. It's called AI Day. And once it arrives, it will rapidly usher in a new age.

For decades, the concept of a man-made intelligence matching or surpassing our own — technically called AGI (artificial general intelligence) or Strong AI — has been steeped in science fiction. Upon hearing the term AI, many people immediately think of the sentient computer HAL in Stanley Kubrick's masterpiece film *2001: A Space Odyssey*. However, what most people fail to grasp is that once AI becomes self-aware and joins with the internet, it could grow its intelligence thousands of times in just mere days, perhaps hours. Frankly, it could quickly surpass all measurements of intelligence that humans are even capable of monitoring and recognizing.

"I think that Ray Kurzweil's estimate that we will achieve human-level

Artificial General Intelligence by around 2029 is a reasonable guesstimate," says Dr. Ben Goertzel.

Originally a math PhD, Goertzel is now a multidisciplinary scientist, author, and entrepreneur. He currently serves as chief scientist of Hong Kong financial firm Aidyia Holdings, chairman of the Artificial General Intelligence Society, and leader of the OpenCog AGI project.

"It could take longer than 2029," Goertzel continues, "if economic troubles prevail or technical problems prove thornier than anticipated. On the other hand, I also think a concerted and well-funded effort by the right people could make it happen before 2020."

Some religious people, anti-transhumanists, and neo-Luddites complain that an advanced AI will rapidly destroy human civilization. In my novel *The Transhumanist Wager*, the evangelical antagonist philosophizes that the first AI will naturally evolve into the Antichrist and bring Armageddon. Most scientists, technologists, and artificial intelligence experts find those worries laughable. Most of them think that AI will usher in a new age of scientific discovery, medical advancement, and technological sophistication only imagined before in science fiction. Some philosophers and futurists think that within the first few years of advanced AI appearing, it will expand learning so far that all important science, technology, and engineering texts will need to be completely rewritten.

The challenge of the human species is to not let this kind of AI get beyond our controls; to have adequate safety measures and kill-switches built in. Such measures would not be dissimilar from how civilization delicately handles nuclear weaponry, which some political experts believe have staved off world wars in the last half-century.

The human race's other challenge is how to merge directly with AI, to discover the technology and build apparatuses to connect our brain's neural networks directly into such an intelligent machine.

Regardless what happens in the future, it's safe to say AI will not be an entity speaking to us in hackneyed parables, or telling us to pluck out our eyes and cut off our hands if we sin. It probably also won't threaten us with a hopeless fiery hell of eternal punishment for our lack of faith. It's far more likely the greatest tool our species has ever created will tell us how to end world poverty with inventive technologies, how to best fix the Earth of the environmental degradation we've caused, and how to heal ourselves of all disease and live indefinitely via radical science. Sure, there will be risks in keeping AI our friend and ally, but there will be even greater rewards in harnessing it and using it to advance civilization.

One thing is for sure, to the human species, the birth of an advanced artificial intelligence will become far more important than the birth of Christ. Christmas, if it survives at all, will be relegated to just another commercial and cultural holiday that superstores and big business thrive on. Meanwhile, reasonable people will celebrate AI Day, the real moment in history the savior of civilization was born.

****

27) Mind Uploading Will Replace God

I hear a lot of philosophical complaints suggesting that being alive in a computer as an uploaded version of oneself is quite different than being alive in the physical world. While that is open for debate, one aspect of the issue people often forget about is that the so-called spirit world of Abrahamic faiths—which approximately four billion people follow—is based on something at least as odd as the bits in software code that will make up any virtual existence.

When you think about it, trying to wrap your brain around how digital technology and all its wonders are even possible is simply bizarre. Only a tiny fraction of the world's population understand such things in any depth. And an even smaller amount of people actually know how to design and create the microchips, circuit boards, and software that constitutes this stuff in the real world. Human beings are a species dependent on a tech-imbued lifestyle that none of us really understand, but accept wholeheartedly as we go on endlessly texting, Facebooking, and video conferencing.

As a non-engineer atheist grappling with the implications of 1s and 0s manifesting all digital reality, I have at least this much in common with religious people—because they can't understand the spirit world either, even if they insist it exists.

The major difference between the religious spirit world and the digital world is that engineers—technology's high priests—can recreate software, microchips, and virtual environments again and again. They can also test, view, change, manipulate, and most importantly, improve upon their creations. They can apply the scientific method and be assured that the worlds they built of bits and code exist—as surely as we know the Earth is spinning, even if we can't feel it.

People of the planet's major religions can't do this with their spirit worlds. They can only make leaps of faith, and elaborately describe it to you. One either agrees or disagrees with them. Amazingly, proof is not necessary to them.

Being able to upload our entire minds into a computer is probably just 25-35 years off given Moore's Law and the current trajectory of technology growth and innovation. If we can harness the power of artificial intelligence in the next 15 years, then we might get there quicker, as AI will likely make the research and progress happen far more rapidly. But mind uploading is generally considered possible by experts. After all, humans are just material machines, striving to create other machines that mirror ourselves and desires.

Already, interaction between microchip and the brain are occurring all around the world in the form of cranial implants helping the deaf, blind, and mentally ill. Furthermore, telepathy, accomplished recently by researchers in India and France, is the communication medium of the future. We're just in the infancy of all this, but progress is accelerating. I'm looking forward to having an exact copy of myself online one day, both as a companion and as a form of personal immortality in case my biological self dies.

Atheists may not believe in God, but as Sam Harris' recent bestseller, *Waking Up: A Guide to Spirituality Without Religion* points out, we are still deeply spiritual creatures, searching for answers, trying to do good upon the world, and pondering the mysteries of the universe. All this is very healthy, and not that different than some core hopes of the religious-minded. In fact, the only real difference between religious people and atheists is the fact that religious people insist an all-knowing deity is outside of themselves and controlling the shape of the world. Atheists see no God and believe unconscious universal forces and human will are responsible for the shape of the world.

It's that shape of the world that I care about. It's that shape that affects our lives and gives form to our society, nations, and deeds. For millennia, society has been controlled, guided, and manipulated by religion—often for the worse. As a rule, the more fundamental a particular religion was, the better it steered its populace in the direction the leaders of the religion wanted. I often refer to this steering as baggage culture, pieces of social structure, cultural conditioning, and archaic rules passed on from generation to generation with little philosophical change or growth, despite the fact that society evolves every year. Eventually, such baggage culture weighs us down so much that society becomes lethargic and hopelessly burdened with nonsense in its many actions. This can be seen in the United State's monopolistic two-party pretend democracy system. It can also be seen in Islam—one of the world's fastest growing religions—whose main sacred text, the Koran, is often seen as being at odds with basic modern day women's rights. Of course, one of the most embarrassing examples of baggage culture I know of is America's Imperial measurement system, which favors obfuscation instead of the better metric system.

So what can we do to eliminate our baggage culture? I'm afraid that little will happen as long as we are exclusively biological. Our instincts for vice, petty behavior, and superstition are too strong. There has certainly been a shift towards moral fortitude, reason, and irreligiosity in many developed countries, but it is slow, very slow. The sad truth is we'll be uploading ourselves into machines long before rationality and agnosticism become truly dominant on Earth. The good news, though, is as people begin uploading themselves, they'll also be hacking and writing improved code for their new digital selves—resulting in "real time evolution" for individuals and the species. It's likely this influx of better code will eliminate lots of things that, historically speaking, religion has attempted to protect people from—namely stupidity and social evil.

Take Andreas Lubitz, the co-pilot who likely intentionally crashed Germanwings Flight 9525 in the Swiss Alps, tragically killing all the people aboard. Lubitz is suspected to have been suffering from depression. In the future, we may all have avatars—perfectly uploaded versions of ourselves existing in the cloud or in chip implants in our brains—and these avatars will help guide us and not allow us to do dumb or terrible things. In the Germanwings plane incident, the avatar would have been able to eliminate the depression in itself, and then could've conveyed that to the other, real life self. In this way, the better suited person would've have been given the task of flying the plane.

This may serve what Abraham Lincoln called the better angels of our nature, which we all have but often don't use. Now, with digital clones participating in our every move, someone trustworthy will always be in our head, advising us of the best path to take. Think of it in terms of a spiritual trainer—or even guru—leading us to be the best we can be.

A good metaphor or comparison of this type of digital assistance will already be happening in the next few years when driverless cars hit the road. In the same way driverless cars will help lessen drunk driving, perfected uploaded avatars will also lead us to be more judicious, moral, and reasonable in our lives.

This is why the future will be far better than it is now. In the coming digital world, we may be perfect, or very close to it. Expect a much more utopian society for whatever social structures end up existing in virtual reality and cyberspace. But also expect the real world to radically improve. Expect the drug user to have their addictions corrected or overcome. Expect the domestic abuser to have their violence and drive for power diminished. Expect the mentally depressed to become happy. And finally, expect the need for religion to disappear as a real-life god—our near perfect moral selves—symbiotically commune with us. In this way, the promising future of atheism and its power will reside in achieving this amazing transhumanist technology. Code, computers, and science will one day replace formal religion and its God, and we will be better as a species for it.

****

28) Upgrading Religion for the 21st Century: Christianity is Forcibly Evolving to Cope with Science and Progress

Recently, the pope made history when he told his flock to accept divorced Catholics. A month later, NPR reported a gay preacher had been ordained as a Baptist minister. Next year it might well be evangelicals in the deep South turning pro-choice. Everywhere around us, traditional Christian theology and its culture is breaking down in hopes of remaining relevant. The reality is with incredible scientific breakthroughs in the 21st century, ubiquitous information via the Internet, and an increasingly nonreligious youth, formal religion has to adapt to survive.

But can it do so without becoming obsolete? Perhaps more importantly, can Christianity — the world's largest religion with 2 billion believers — remain the overarching societal power it's been for millennia? The answer is not an easy one for the old faith-driven guard.

To remain a dominant force throughout the 21st century, formal religion will have to bend. It will have to adapt. It will have to evolve. Hell, it will have to be upgraded. Welcome to the growing impact of Christian relativism.

The familiar term cultural relativism was coined by anthropologist Franz Baos, who suggested that people have a difficult time understanding another's culture without having grown up in it—so therefore we should strive to empathize more with foreign cultures and people. It's a great concept, and after many years reporting for National Geographic in dozens of countries, I came to strongly believe in the idea.

Christian relativism, however, does not have that honor of generating empathy so easily—at least not until it separates itself from its cornerstone philosophy: adherence to the Bible. Even with its many dozens of translations, most everything in the Bible simply cannot be logically interpreted in a multitude of ways—or flippantly passed over in generous empathy. To make the Bible's deity-approved instructions and ideas soundly work, church leaders pushing Christian relativism may simply have to back down or say it made a mistake with its past fundamentalism.

For example, if the Bible clearly says being gay is a sin (and it does many times), then Christians can't just wake up one day and say homosexuality is permissible without dismissing God's word. Another example is women; if the Bible says they can't be priests and must submit to men, then the church can never profess to believe in equality—which is does all the time. Additionally, if committing blasphemy (striving to become god-like) through transhumanism is an unforgiveable sin that leads to eternal punishment, then Christians can't say they represent a loving and kind God. The hypocrisy is too much to pretend one is being logical or reasonable—since transhumanists vocally aim to never die and possibly even become gods (or God) through science and technology.

This is the dilemma that the Abrahamic religious face in the age of Christian relativism. They have sealed themselves in the ideological fort for protection, and now they have no way out without atheists and agnostics chiding them. Language is fiercely mechanical— and in the case of the Bible, many of the truths are prominently black and white.

The antithesis of the Bible is, of course, the much simpler Western ideology: the scientific method, upon which the other part of modern humanity's culture was built upon—the one that brought us skyscrapers, CRISPR gene editing tech, robots, and vaccinations so our children don't die from measles. The scientific method states nothing is black and white, but if you prove something enough times, it's safe to trust it until something strange or unwanted occurs. It's humble at its core, unlike Christianity which claims to be under guidance of an omnipotent God.

Consider Christianity's core message: You are born in sin, and only through Christ can you be redeemed and reach a happy afterlife. The scientific method would've never entertained such a conclusion, because it would've been stuck asking what is sin?, and where is Christ? — neither of which can be proven one way or the other.

With this in mind, how does Christian relativism then expect to be taken seriously? I wish that was the question, but people are so entrenched into Judeo-Christian culture, that we rarely consider that Christianity is even changing. We only think we are becoming more open-minded, and that God and our religious brethren should pat us on the back for our newfound wisdom.

While I shake my head in disbelief at the Christian mirage all around me (and the billion people who call the pope wonderfully progressive despite his disdain of condoms and other birth control), I accept it as a better fate that the far more dogmatic one humans endured in the 20th Century. I believe I speak for the one billion nonreligious people out there when I say I'll take progress however I can get it — even if it results in a Jesus Singularity, where even the superintelligent robots engineers are trying to make may end up being programmed to believe in Christ. But Christian relativism is not a cure to the disease—it's just a band-aid of belief. The cure — or better put: the sobering tonic—is the scientific method, a simple philosophy that says: Get used to not knowing anything for sure — then make up your own mind on what you believe.

****

29) Are We Heading for a Jesus Singularity?

As an atheist transhumanist, I dislike the idea of mixing religion with transhumanism. The two ideas go together as much as a computer chip goes with a medieval torture rack. Religion is based on faith and archaic dogmatic tradition. Transhumanism — the concept of moving beyond the human being using science and technology — is based on reason and scientific evolutionary principles. Yet, the two viewpoints may be inextricably joined more than either side cares to admit.

Many experts expect scientists to develop artificial general intelligence (AGI) — intelligence equivalent to human beings — sometime in the next 20 years. It's likely within a few months of AGI arriving it will independently upgrade itself into something monumentally more intelligent and complex than humans. It'll be up to society to carefully control this dangerous process and avoid a Terminator-like scenario. Some futurists and technologists believe the beginning of AGI is the beginning of the Singularity, a concept where intelligence and technology grow at exponential speeds and human life is forever transformed.

The question of whether civilization is heading for a Jesus Singularity should begin with a head count of the admitted atheists in the U.S. Congress. The count doesn't take long. Currently, the number is an astonishing zero. That means all 535 members leading our government are religious (or pretending to be religious). Now add the fact that human lives are getting longer — much longer if you're a congressperson with access to the best modern medicine — and the reality is that many of the religious-minded people in government control (especially without term limits) will not be losing control anytime soon.

While not guaranteed, it's probable AGI will be born somewhere in California's Silicon Valley, where many of the planet's best computer engineers and programmers live. Mountain View-based Google, one of the wealthiest companies in the world, is leading the charge and sinking millions of dollars into AI projects. Cupertino-based Apple, with its juvenile AI star Siri, is another player in AGI development mode. Dozens of start-ups and the U.S. government are also working on creating sophisticated thinking machines.

All this begs the question, if AGI will be here in 20 years or so, and most of those people currently in charge of the U.S. government subscribe to Christianity and believe in Jesus, what are atheist transhumanists to do?

On the surface, a Jesus Singularity seems comical, fit for a Monty Python movie. It contradicts many of the core beliefs of science, reason, and why a Singularity could happen in the first place. Or does it?

Perhaps the first AGI will become the Second Coming of Christ, as detailed in Revelations in the bible. Could the first AGI be programmed with a Jesus-in-the-box attitude and become a Judeo-Christian-minded God, an all-powerful entity who believes it died for our sins and wants to make us its loving followers? Maybe there will be some in Congress who insist the U.S. government attempt to convert the first AGI entity to Christianity. Sound crazy? I'm willing to bet most members of Congress have done that exact thing with their children. Why should the potentially most powerful being ever created be spared the same fate? Even the Pope has argued that if aliens came to Earth, we should convert them to Christians.

Of course, another alternative for the planet's future, as antagonist Reverend Belinas in my philosophical novel *The Transhumanist Wager* prophesizes, is the first AGI will become the Antichrist, setting off a terrible chain of events for civilization that will end with Armageddon.

Either way, it appears the nonreligious minority of the planet will not change the attitudes of the world's religious majority before the Singularity occurs. Logic therefore dictates that transhumanists and atheists remain more open to working with formal religion and their leaders than first thought. Many of those faith-oriented politicians may still be in office in 20 years when all-important decisions must be made about civilization's expected digital future.

For many transhumanists, survival is the first and foremost part of why we are transhumanists. We want to live indefinitely using transhumanist science and technology. We may complain that we live in a highly religious world full of irrational dogma, ritual, and holidays, but it would be more irrational to stop a Singularity just because a "divine avatar" wears a digital crown of thorns and preaches goodwill to our neighbors.

Given an either-or choice, I would rather live forever in a Jesus Singularity than die or be left behind because I wouldn't accept it — especially since the best part about a Jesus Singularity is I can remain a grinning atheist through it all.

****

30) A Brain Implant that Registers Trauma Could Help Prevent Rape, Tragedy, and Crime—So Why Don't We Have it Yet?

There's been a lot of talk across America about college rape culture in the last few weeks. Much major media has been highlighting the persistent and unfortunate problem. Perhaps the most well-known article came from *Rolling Stone*, which ran a highly controversial story highlighting seven University of Virginia fraternity students allegedly raping one freshman girl for hours during a party. In the wake of so much arresting coverage, numerous universities and legislative bodies are considering new methods to deal with the problem.

So far, those new methods seem to consist mostly of advocating for clearer language to stop the violence from happening in the first place and greater transparency in the rape victim's reporting process. I'm not optimistic the changes will do much to stop rape and other forms of criminal violence in any significant way. There are too many aggressive, idiotic men out there—and yes, men are almost always responsible for the violence.

The facts of domestic abuse in America are sobering. Nonprofit Arkansas Coalition Against Domestic Violence reports that every 15 seconds a woman is beaten and that 35 percent of all emergency room visits are a result of domestic violence. Nonprofit A.A.R.D.V.A.R.C., An Abuse, Rape, and Domestic Violence Aid and Resource Collection, reports that that the US Surgeon General states that domestic violence is the leading cause of injury to women between the ages of 15 and 44 in the United States. According to *Feminist.com*, over 22 million women in the United States have been raped in their lifetime, based on the National Intimate Partner and Sexual Violence Survey 2010. SafeHorizon, the largest victims' service agency in America, says there are 2.9 million reports of child abuse every year nationally, and it costs $124 billion dollars annually in medical, court, law enforcement, child welfare, and juvenile protection services to deal with the problem.

As a transhumanist, I strive to consider all societal problems from technological and scientific points of views. It turns out there might be a simple solution that could reduce rape and some violent crime all across the country. I call it the trauma alert implant.

Cranial implants and brain wave technology—despite a Mark of the Beast reputation by Christian conspiracy theorists—have come a long way in the last few years. Already, hundreds of thousands of people in the world have microchip implants in their heads, consisting of everything from chips to help Parkinson's sufferers to cochlear implants for the deaf to devices to assist Alzheimer's patients with memory loss. For each, this technology allows a better life. DARPA recently announced a $70 million dollar five-year plan to develop implants that can monitor soldier's health. It's part of President Obama's new multi-billion dollar BRAIN Initiative.

Implants using Electroencephalography (EEG) technology can read and decipher brain waves. Trauma, however experienced, is a measurable biological phenomenon that can be monitored and captured by an implant device. Scientists must do nothing more than create a trackable chip that sends an emergency signal to nearby authorities when it registers extreme trauma. Help can then arrive quickly to the victim.

Much of the technology for such a device basically already exists. And such a device could be useful for far more than rape or criminal violence, too. Drowning, being burned in a fire, automobile accidents, building collapses, snake bites, kidnappings, bullet wounds, senior citizens who've fallen down stairs and can't get up—the list of terrible things that happen to humans goes on and on. The result of every one of them is almost always the same: brain waves that manifest extreme trauma—the human's most basic response and alert system. Regardless what misfortune happens to a human being, most experts agree that getting victims rapid emergency assistance is the single best way to help them.

Consider the 2-year-old boy was snatched away from its parents by an alligator at Walt Disney World in 2016. I have a similar-aged toddler myself, and I followed this heartbreaking story closely. Unfortunately, it ended as horribly as it began, with the recovery of a dead child.

While scene reports claim the father got into the water to save his son, perhaps if that 2-year-old at Disney World had been GPS chipped, the parents could have tracked him on their smartphones. And security might have been able to quickly identify his location in the water, perhaps even fast enough to have rescued him. *The New York Times* reports that the body was tragically found underwater only 10-15 feet from where it was last seen.

That's of little consolation now, of course, and I don't mean to be insensitive to the family's loss, but I do think this tragedy illustrates how implants could help improve public safety. They could help track our children, and adults for that matter, in the case of kidnapping and Amber alerts, or even just when they get lost on a hike in the woods.

As the father of a 5-year-old who will be attending school next year, I'm a big believer in the future that all children will get chipped somewhere on their bodies, perhaps like all children get vaccines in the U.S. It's crazy to me that we don't develop and use this technology, especially with our children. I'm looking into getting my children chipped after this alligator incident and because, as a controversial presidential candidate, I have security issues myself to worry about.

Of course, it's not only implants. It's chip tattoos, GPS jewelry, wearable tech T-shirts, or even shoes with tracking tech built into them. Using tech to keep humanity safe is a burgeoning field. Interestingly, an industry already exists around children using tech to keep their whereabouts safe, but they're mostly children with disabilities—some who have a propensity to wander off.

Perhaps the most advanced case of chipping people already in existence has to do with the military. Reports describe special forces experimenting with them so they can be tracked. In 2014, for example, the U.S. Department of Defense announced a $26 million grant for a brain implant that would record, analyze, and potentially alter live electrical signals to soldiers. The military is getting so interested in implants that I was recently asked to consult for the U.S. Navy on research of chipping their service people.

Back to the trauma alert implant—which to me is the holy grail of safety. Another great thing about it is that not everyone would have to get it to help stop violent crime and domestic abuse. In fact, probably most people wouldn't (though, I surmise in the future many people will get one for a multitude of reasons). The existence of the chip itself—similar to a possible hidden camera in a room—would be enough to scare off many criminals, who would always be second guessing if their victim had one. This would especially be the case when it comes to crimes that are hard to prove or go habitually unreported, such as date rape.

All things considered, the trauma alert implant sounds like a sensible and impressive thing. So why don't we have them yet?

To begin with, Americans are wary of brain implants. They don't mind holding a cell phone to their ears for a half hour, but ask them to get a piece of sophisticated tech inside their heads and many freak out. They squawk how weird it is and that they don't want to be a cyborg (all the while spending untold hours surfing the internet, flying on jet airplanes 30,000 feet in the air, and taking multiple vaccines and pills). The transhumanist age is already here, whether it's weird or not. For most people, it's just a matter of culturally accepting it.

Another complaint that people have with implants is the privacy issue. Nobody wants to be trackable. Sure, that's understandable. But bear in mind, that every time you get on the internet, stop at a gas station, or use your credit card, you're already being tracked. We may all distrust surveillance, but that's not going to stop the gargantuan amount of cameras recording in America right now, many of them in public places. While solid information is hard to find on how many cameras are operating in America, Wikipedia reports that Chicago has at least 10,000, and the United Kingdom may have as many 4.2 million cameras, or 1 for every 14 people. The good news is, just like our cell phones we carry around, we'll likely have the option to turn off our implants anytime we want, thereby giving us control of who can watch us. Additionally, surely implants could be programmed so that they could "only" be tracked once they were triggered for extreme trauma.

But probably the most significant reason Americans dislike implants is because of religion. At least 80 percent of the country's population holds some form of faith—mostly of Christian denomination. And a significant number of Christian people consider brain implant technology to be the definitive Mark of the Beast—and a sign of End Times. I'm an agnostic tending towards atheism, so I don't understand those fears. But I do know that Revelations and the Second Coming of Jesus supposedly can't be stopped by people, according to the Bible, so perhaps Americans should work through their cyborg-phobias and embrace useful transhumanist technology. After all, if a gang of rape perpetrators suspected their victim had a trauma alert chip that would notify authorities, do you think they'd still commit the crime? Surely most wouldn't, especially not university students.

I'm grateful my young daughters will probably never have to worry about drunk drivers on their prom night. In a decade's time, most cars on the road in America will be driverless or come with alcohol detection systems that don't allow inebriated drivers. Such technological innovation is just a drop in the ocean of the benefits that progress brings to our world. The truth is that technology can help fix almost all the world's problems. It can also help with the tragedy of rape and criminal violence, which dramatically harms nearly 10,000 women and children a day in the US. If even a small portion of the population would have trauma alert implants, rape and criminal violence might be substantially reduced.

******

CHAPTER VI: CULTURAL EVOLUTION

31) Watch Out Cupid! Transhumanism is Going to Change Love

I've received a lot of advice on romantic love over the years. It seems everyone is an expert on it and has something to say. Most of the advice I received was from my close guy friends, a bunch of professional, weekend warrior types. Unfortunately, most of their advice was biased towards getting the so-called hot girl, and then later in life: the trophy wife (hot girl who can be a good mother).

It was poor advice. In terms of courting women, my guy friends and most males—regardless of education, class differences, ethnicity, or career—are just plain dummies when it comes to finding the right mate. They think in archaic ways, driven by flashy, peacock-inspired propensities that worked for our primate ancestors, but hardly fill modern-day needs successfully. Those ways never worked much for me, and in light of the coming transhumanist era, they work even less.

I met my wife through online dating, which is perhaps the single greatest sociological invention of the late 20th Century. My wife didn't have a picture as part of her profile, which is what attracted me to her. She had initials behind her name, though, and I found them sexy. When I married her less than a year later, she was almost 40, three years older than me. Even though my friends liked and respected her, they thought I was nuts. She was too old, they cautioned. Even my parents were worried, wondering if she was beyond the permissible breeding age. I was warned of having a child with three eyes and fish gills—that is, if we could get pregnant at all. My wife and I now have two gorgeous kids, and those sexy initials behind her name haven't aged a day.

How many men in the world have met a spectacular woman, but because she's beyond the nebulous, culturally accepted age of bearing children, she has been strung along, eventually judged, and then dumped? I can think of numerous instances with my guy friends, who seem stuck on landing the perfectly fresh 20-something-year-old, even at the expense of personality, soul, experience, and respect. In case my friends haven't been paying attention, human evolution is occurring faster than ever. In vitro fertilization (IVF), genetic engineering, and cytoplasm donation are changing the way we mate and build families, and it's doing it for the betterment of society.

Though hard to believe, the reality is simple: It's likely going to be safer and easier for a 70-year-old woman to have healthy offspring in two decades time than it is for a 25-year-old to have offspring today. In 20 years, many babies in America will be designer children, with genetic traits, sex, and emotional tendencies picked out ahead of time. Ectogenesis, raising a fetus in an artificial womb outside the body, will also likely be available. In fact, even men will be able to give birth to children via surgically implanted uteruses if they want. But even more far out, different sexes may not even be needed at all, based on advancing cloning technologies.

However, that's just the start of the transhumanist era upon us. Let's play a thought-experiment: Remember that amazing person you once met who was 20 or 30 years older than you—the one you clicked perfectly with on so many levels and who totally inspired you. If that person can live a few more decades, he or she is going to be able to come back into their prime via reverse aging. And plastic surgery, whether vane or not, is going to make them look better than they've ever looked before. Indeed, the game of dating and romantic love is about to be dramatically upgraded. The old rules of courtship and relationships will soon crumble.

Leading gerontologist Aubrey de Grey, chief scientist and co-founder of Silicon Valley-based SENS Research Foundation, believes we may be able to stop aging in humans in about 20 years. Researchers have already had success with this in mice. Most laypeople don't realize how far longevity science has come in the last few decades. That's why Google just started the company Calico and is putting a billion dollars into aging research and the ability to conquer human mortality. Achieving such scientific milestones are the inevitable future, and they will create a paradigm shift for the species. Getting old will simply not be a part of life for transhumanity. Perfect health and living in one's prime age will be the ultimate desired goal.

So the next time you're in a coffee shop, don't overlook that 70-year-old sitting in the corner reading Dickens, Hemmingway, or maybe even a copy of *The Transhumanist Wager*. That senior citizen with their years of wisdom and experience might soon be fair game for a love interest.

****

32) Marriage Won't Make Sense When We Live 1000 Years

I was jubilant the US Supreme Court ruled in favor of gay marriage. Events that lead to more freedom and equality are positive progress.

However, what doesn't seem to be making the news is the fact that marriage—especially to many young people—isn't as attractive as it once was.

There are a number of reasons for this. People want to focus on their careers, not spouses. Getting married and having a traditional wedding costs a lot of money (besides, around 40 percent of those who wed will go through at least one divorce in their lives, causing potential harm to their ideals, children, and finances). Finally, having kids out of wedlock is becoming more socially acceptable.

But there's another reason that is increasingly relevant. It has to do with transhumanism. In the transhumanist age of extended lifespans, where many people will live beyond 100 years of age, the question of being married until "death does us part" has real consequence.

In America most marriages last about a decade. However, it's safe to say that plenty of those marriages that do last much longer are not entirely happy or fulfilling. Fear of being alone, apathy, and finances often bind the reluctant wedlock yoke. But I believe the primary reason people stay married when they're not happy is religion. Some Abrahamic religions treat divorce as sin (thereby potentially jeopardizing one's afterlife if you get divorced). Especially in America where some 80 percent of the citizenry is Christian, faith plays an influential part in promoting marital union.

Social, financial, and religions pressures aside, the deeper philosophical question of the transhumanist age is: Are people really willing to marry for the rest of their lives when those lives may be hundreds or even thousands of years long? This is especially a pertinent question when it's almost certain coming technology will allow us to radically change who we are in the near future, both physically and mentally.

In a world of indefinite lifespans, the marriage commitment takes on a whole new meaning and level of commitment.

America and many parts of the developed world are losing their religion, however, which certainly will contribute to less social pushing for matrimony. A recent Pew Research Center study found that many young people increasingly possess no religious leanings at all. In just a few decade's time, if this statistical trajectory holds, younger generations may broadly prefer not to ever marry.

And who can argue with them? Within 15 years, some of the so-called classic advantages of marriage will be gone. Many people will have robot house nannies, driverless cars, and automated stoves that cook for us. In 20 years' time, we may also use artificial wombs (ectogenesis) to grow babies, and use our own stem cells to provide genetic treatments to build the perfect child. A spouse will simply not be as necessary in the transhumanist age as it once was.

Naysayers will argue that only a wholesome, traditional family can produce good, well-rounded children. But that's deeply wrong. In 15 to 20 years' time, cranial implant technology will enable humans to overcome many of their idiosyncrasies and bad behaviors—making a new generation of very wholesome and exemplary children. In fact, going to college may be replaced by downloading higher educations into our brains.

Even morality may be built in by personal avatars that are always looking over our shoulder for us, not dissimilar to what Abraham Lincoln called the "better angels of our nature." In just over a decade, traditional family life and the institution of marriage as we know it will face the largest disruption it's ever gone through.

And sex? Well, that can and will be better and more pleasurable with the rise of transhumanist technology. Already, scientists are working on pure, outright stimulation of the erogenous zones in our brains. Stimulating this part of ourselves will be easier, on-demand, and disease and pregnancy-free. Of course, the coming world of virtual and augmented reality will also offer endless amounts of physical experimentation via haptic suits to satisfy one's lusts, too.

Another thing sure to make people—both young and old—wary of marriage in the future is the growing promise of gender-identity choice. In the transhumanist age, we are not stuck being males or females, but whatever version we want—maybe even something between or combined. Transgender surgery is catching on and people can change themselves as they see fit, or they can do it just for kicks and new experiences. In fact, most of the modern medicine, surgery techniques, and tech are already here today or coming soon—complete with augmented penises, vaginas, and other sexual body parts that we can replace or modify.

But the bigger transhumanist steps of gender and identity will come when we begin uploading our minds into machines, and people must decide what their avatars will be like. Surely, many people will experiment with other sides of themselves they always wondered about. Think of uploading as an anonymous masquerade party, where you can be anything you want, and then be something else later that day. People may change their genders daily, depending on who they interact with or how they feel.

All this radical tech and change the human race is about to undergo means one thing: marriage is heading the way of the dinosaurs. So instead of celebrating our rights of matrimony for gay people or trying to privatize it for tax and liberty reasons, maybe we should also begin endorsing the phasing out of marriage from society's mindset.

Of course, that doesn't mean we won't have intimate relationships that are deep and meaningful. It just means that the multi-millennial-old institution of marriage—began by our ancestors to transfer inheritance in the form of dowries (often weapons and livestock)—has increasingly less relevance today. In the meantime, we'll come up with new ways to create legal structures to protect relationships and those we love in a deeply litigious society. In nearly every instance of legal companionship, a simple notarized document giving permission to a partner can serve where a marriage certificate once did the same. In the future, this legal procedure won't be physical, anyway, but notaries and permissions will be done by large database scans of retinas, fingerprints, and DNA samples on your smartphone or chip implants.

Even though I'm a happily married man with two kids, I'm all too aware of how society, the government, and especially religion has sold people on the concept that love needs to be institutionalized and consummated by legal marital vows.

In my opinion, that's all just another level of control someone or some entity is trying to put over me and others. If one is in love, then they need no controls. Love just is, and for two people in love, it manifests itself every day. And if it doesn't, then it's no longer love. Society can operate on a new social structure that incorporates other versions of social bonding, ones that also support a strong, caring, and connected society. This includes stepping away from all-holy monogamy, and implementing a larger mindset about what constitutes relationships.

For the record, I'm not saying let's throw away marriage. But let's stop society and government from promoting it like it's the only way to love and exist.

In the transhumanist age, it's time to leave behind closed-mindedness. In our relationships with others, we should instead look not with our biases and bigotry, but for what a person we care about can do for us, and what we can do for them. That person may be a human, a cyborg, a robot, or even a computer program. Whatever it is, frankly, is not important. It's what it does and how it does it. And if it does good, honest, and meaningful actions, then that's plenty upon which to build love, intimacy, and a successful future.

In fact, soon, the next civil rights debate of love and marriage will probably involve whether we can wed the coming generation of intelligent robots and avatars, which may be nearly as smart as us in a decade's time. This brings up larger questions of different legalities. It also brings up polygamy. Is being wed to two robots at the same time more socially acceptable then marrying two human spouses? Will the US government support tax breaks of marrying robots as it does for humans (as President, I would advocate for this)? Will divorce laws be different for the machines we wed—assuming they'll agree to wed us at all. Will divorces be governed by communal law or common law? Do we need consent to marry a machine? We surely don't need any to fall in love with one.

The coming transhumanist age is indubitably thorny. The onslaught of radically technology in our lives is challenging the very institutions and ideas we have built society upon. However, I hold much hope that technology will continue to allow us to live longer, better, and freer. Whatever happens, we shouldn't remain mired in past practices that once served society, but no longer do in such a positive or functional manner. We must look forward and search out new ways of living that grant us improved livelihoods.

****

33) Programming Hate into AI Will be Controversial, but Probably Necessary

In the last few years, the topic of artificial intelligence (AI) has been thrust into the mainstream. No longer just the domain of sci-fi fans, nerds or Google engineers, I hear people discussing AI at parties, coffee shops and even at the dinner table: My five-year-old daughter brought it up the other night over taco lasagna. When I asked her if anything interesting had happened in school, she replied that her teacher discussed smart robots.

The exploration of intelligence — be it human or artificial — is ultimately the domain of epistemology, the study of knowledge. Since the first musings of creating AI back in antiquity, epistemology seems to have led the debate on how to do it. The question I hear most in this field from the public is: How can humans develop another intelligent consciousness if we can't even understand our own?

It's a prudent question. The human brain, despite being only about three pounds in weight, is the least understood organ in the body. And with a billion neurons — with 100 trillion connections — it's safe to say it's going to be a long time before we end up figuring out the brain.

Generally, scientists believe human consciousness is a compilation of many chemicals in the brain forced though a prism that produces cognitive awareness designed to insist an entity is aware of not only itself but also the outside world.

Some people argue that the quintessential key to consciousness is awareness. French philosopher and mathematician René Descartes may have made the initial step by saying: I think, therefore I am. But thinking does not adequately define consciousness. Justifying thinking is much closer to the meaning that's adequate. It really should be: I believe I'm conscious, therefore I am.

But even awareness doesn't ring right with me when searching for a grand theory of consciousness. We can teach a robot all day to insist it is aware, but we can't teach it to prove it's not a brain in a vat — something people still can't do either.

Christof Koch, chief neuroscientist at the Allen Institute for Brain Science, offers a more unique and holistic version of consciousness. He thinks consciousness can happen in any complex processing system, including animals, worms and possibly even the Internet.

In an interview, when asked what consciousness is, Koch replied, "There's a theory, called Integrated Information Theory, developed by Giulio Tononi at the University of Wisconsin, that assigns to any one brain, or any complex system, a number — denoted by the Greek symbol Φ — that tells you how integrated a system is, how much more the system is than the union of its parts. Φ gives you an information-theoretical measure of consciousness. Any system with integrated information different from zero has consciousness. Any integration feels like something."

If Koch and Tononi are correct, then it would be a mistake to ever think one conscious could equal another. It would be apples and oranges. Just like no snowflake or planet is the same as another, we must be on our guard against using anthropomorphic prejudice when thinking about consciousness.

In this way, the first autonomous super-intelligence we create via machines may think and behave dramatically different than us — so much so that it may not ever relate to us, or vice versa. In fact, every AI we ever create in the future may leave us in very short order for distant parts of the digital universe — an ego-thumping concept made visual in the brilliant movie Her. Of course, an AI might just terminate itself, too, upon realizing it's alive and surrounded by curious humans peering at it.

Whatever happens, in the same way there is the anthropological concept cultural relativism, we must be ready for "consciousness relativism" — the idea that one consciousness may be totally different than another, despite the hope that math, logic and coding will be obvious communication tools.

This makes even more sense when you consider how small-minded humans and their consciousness might actually be. After all, nearly all our perception comes from our five senses, which is how our brain makes sense of the world. And every one of our senses is quite poor in terms of possible ability. The eye, for example, only sees about 1 percent of the universe's light spectrum.

For this reason, I'm reluctant to insist on consciousness being one thing or the other, and do lean toward believing Koch and Tononi are correct by saying variations of consciousness can be seen in many forms across the spectrum of existence.

This also reinforces why I'm reluctant to believe that AI will fundamentally be like us. I surmise it may learn to replicate our behavior — perhaps even perfectly — but it will always be something different. Replication is no different than the behavior of a wind-up doll. Most humans hope for much more of themselves and their consciousness. And, of course, most AI engineers want much more for the machines they hope to give a conscious rise to.

Despite that, we will still try to create AI with our own values and ways of thinking, including imbuing it with traits we possess. If I had to pinpoint one behavioral trait of consciousness that humans all have and should also be instilled in AI, it would be empathy. It's empathy that will form the type of AI consciousness the world wants and needs — and one that people also can understand and accept.

On the other hand, if a created consciousness can empathize, then it must also be able to like or dislike — and even to love or hate something.

Therein lies the conundrum. In order for a consciousness to make judgments on value, both liking and disliking (love and hate) functions must be part of the system. No one minds thinking about AI's that can love — but super-intelligent machines that can hate? Or feel sad? Or feel guilt? That's much more controversial — especially in the drone age where machines control autonomous weaponry. And yet, anything less than that coding in empathy to an intelligence just creates a follower machine — a wind-up doll consciousness.

Kevin LaGrandeur, a professor at the New York Institute of Technology, recently wrote, "If a machine could truly be made to 'feel' guilt in its varying degrees, then would we have problems of machine suffering and machine 'suicide'"? If we develop a truly strong artificial intelligence, we might — and then we would face the moral problem of creating a suffering being.

It's a pickle for sure. I don't envy the programmers who are endeavoring to bring a super intelligence into our world, knowing that their creations may also consciously hate things — including its creators. Such programming may just lead to a world where robots and machine intelligences experience the same modern-day problems — angst, bigotry, depression, loneliness and rage — afflicting humanity.

****

34) Is an Affair in Virtual Reality Still Cheating?

I hadn't touched another woman in an intimate way since before getting married six years ago. Then, in the most peculiar circumstances, I was doing it. I was caressing a young woman's hands. I remember thinking as I was doing it: I don't even know this person's name.

After 30 seconds, the experience became too much and I stopped. I ripped off my Oculus Rift headset and stood up from the chair I was sitting on, stunned. It was a powerful experience, and I left convinced that virtual reality was not only the future of sex, but also the future of infidelity.

Okay, I could be wrong. When I told my wife about it, she laughed, saying, "It's a just a software program. It's just a sexy lady made of 1s and 0s appearing real to your visual cortex."

Perhaps my wife is right. However, I couldn't help thinking: What happens when the software seems even more real than the actual thing?

My brush with virtual infidelity came about after giving a speech at WEST, the Wearable, Entertainment & Sports Toronto conference. Companies developing software and programs for the gadgets lined the hallways outside the conference with tables for their products, and they had an excellent array of gadgets on display to play with. I sat down at one run by the company Cinehackers that promised a movie-like experience with the Oculus Rift.

Cinehackers had created a way to let virtual reality users feel like they were in a first-person perspective movie, kind of like *Being John Malcovich*.

Within the first few moments of strapping on their Oculus Rift and earphones, I was immersed into their cinematic programming. It was hard to distinguish that I was looking at a program instead of being in real life. The film that had me holding hands with a young woman is called *I Am You*.

While VR sex has been explored at length, even by people using full-body haptic suits to experience full sexual immersion, the idea of digital infidelity and the confusing moral implications is largely uncharted.

"It makes no difference if the cheating occurred in person or online through the use of porn, webcams, social media, or some other digital technology," said Robert Weiss LCSW, CSAT-S, a therapist and expert on the relationship between digital technology and human sexuality. "A 'virtual world' affair is every bit as painful to a betrayed spouse as an in-the-flesh affair."

That was the typical response from the people I spoke with, but I'm not convinced of that interpretation. Many people in the Western world deem pornography as acceptable to enjoy, partly because they believe it doesn't affect their actual physical world that much. Looking at porn on a computer screen—or a magazine in your bed—is just not really that real. After all, you can't get an STD from your television or get your smartphone screen pregnant. Few except the diehard prudish would insist some kind of moral line is being betrayed. So when does that moral line get crossed? When does one's spouse or partner say enough is enough—you're cheating on me?

Perhaps technological progress will determine that moment, and based on my WEST experience, it might be coming sooner than people think.

Over the next coming decades, virtual sex could alter how we love one another. I see a day coming when people could break up over a partner's desire to use virtual sex as an outlet, whereas in the past, causal porn as we know it today would've been tolerated. This is because virtual sex is so much more powerful—it's truly immersive. And that could scare real life partners off.

Porn has never really attracted me that much, partly because of a story I heard when I was younger, about a chicken that kept trying to mate with a cardboard cutout of a chicken that was dangled in front of it. I could never get the image out of mind that human porn was similar.

But virtual reality is way different than that. Many of the senses are stimulated in life-like ways. And it's going to get way more powerful too, way beyond just visuals. In the future, sex contraptions will become more common, where users dawn haptic suits and other types of technology that help mimic real sexual motions. Of course, speakers can already make people hear auditory moaning. And even sex scents released into the air may one day occur—there is already a company that creates odors for gaming.

The core dilemma of what I experienced in VR in Toronto wasn't just about sex or intimacy. It was about the possibility of finding amazing love so easily. And that's where I think virtual porn will make it challenging for people and couples. A future is upon us where we will be able to intimately bond with near-perfect individuals in VR all the time, one that may even include Hollywood actors or celebrity models, in the case of Cinehackers. We can build castles and paradises with these very real-looking virtual people in Second Life and elsewhere. How will our spouses back in flawed biological flesh ever compete? Will we ever be satisfied again in the physical world? The difficult truth is: maybe not.

Fidelity, for the most the part, has long been a way to preserve a genetic line and keep resources within reach of small group of people. But is that because no other challenge has arisen to fidelity? Many people would say fidelity is not broken with porn use. But what about sex with a life-like robot?

I hear friends tell me all the time that they'll never have sex with a robot. When I ask them why, they have no substantive answer, except to tell me "it doesn't feel right."

This "not feeling right" is a concept that some people call the Uncanny Valley, a concept discussed 40 years ago by a Japanese professor at the Tokyo Institute of Technology about the point where robots that appear human repulse people. However, a growing robotics sex industry, now over many millions of dollars strong seems to counter that argument.

Emma Cott of *The New York Times* recently wrote a story about a sex doll maker that seems to support this: "The creator of the RealDoll says he has sold over 5,000 customizable, life-size dolls since 1996, with prices from $5,000 to $10,000. Not only can his customers decide on body type and skin, hair, and eye color... a craftsman was even furnishing one with custom-ordered toes."

Not that I'm going to be doing this anytime soon, but personally, I feel more comfortable having so-called extramarital sexual liaisons in cyberspace with software than the real world with a robot that calls out my name and asks me how my day went. I think my wife—and the spouses of other people—will feel the same way. For this reason, I don't expect robot sex to become nearly as pervasive as virtual reality sex, which is simpler and less complicated.

Whatever happens, the old rules of fidelity are bound to change dramatically. Not because people are more open or closed-minded, but because evolving technology is about the force the issues into our brains with tantalizing 1s and 0s.

****

35) The Next Step for Veganism Is Ditching Our Bodies and Digitizing Our Minds

144,000,000. That's roughly the number of land animals killed every day to produce meat, dairy, and eggs for human consumption. It's a staggering, horrific number. It's also a number that means billions of more animals are constantly enslaved—many in terrible conditions, suffering throughout their lives, waiting to meet a bloody, often painful death.

No wonder veganism is a quickly-growing worldwide movement. A top priority for vegans is not harming animals. Some of the largest organizations and groups that support or endorse veganism are PETA (People for the Ethical Treatment of Animals), ALF (Animal Liberation Front), and the Humane Society.

The problem is, despite veganism catching on worldwide, the slaughter of more and more animals is inevitable because of an expanding world population. Another problem is that even going totally vegan can carry a cost—sometimes one with a higher animal body count and more environmental damage due to the way the farming industrial complex works. (For example, fertilizer for grains—a worldwide staple—can be made partially from meat products.) So what are vegans to do to stop animal suffering and be better stewards of the planet?

The answer is bewildering—and it probably won't be satisfying to plant-loving people. Nonetheless, it will inevitably eliminate most human-caused animal deaths. The answer is transhumanism—the movement that aims to replace human biology with synthetic and machine parts.

You see, the most important goal of transhumanism is to try to overcome death with science and technology. Most cellular degeneration—otherwise known as aging and sickness—comes from the failing of cells. That failure is at least partially caused by the daily act of eating and drinking—of putting foreign objects into our bodies which cells have to consume or discard to try to create energy. Paraxdoxically, it's stressful and hard work for cells to endlessly do this just to live. A simple way to eliminate this Sisyphean task—all the steaks, chocolate donuts, bacon breakfasts, and even my favorite, scotch—is to get rid of human reliance on food and drink entirely.

Transhumanists, like myself, want to get rid of it all. We want to strip you of your stomach, your guts, and even your anus—and replace it all with machine parts and bionics. In the future, there will be no eating, drinking, or defecation.

The obvious question: Where will we get energy from if we don't eat?

To begin with, we'd need a lot less energy to live since eating, food gathering, and meal preparation take a lot of energy too—even if it's just driving to Taco Bell, Denny's, or visiting the salad bar at Whole Foods.

How we get energy really depends on what humans evolve into over the next 25-50 years—and a lot of that depends on how artificial intelligence unfolds. I already have friends planning in the next 12 months to implant chips onto their brains so they can commune telepathically with machines. And with experts like scientist Ben Goertzel predicting a machine consciousness being here in as little as 15-20 years, there's a possibility we'll be going Matrix-mode shortly after. An uploaded mind will only need electricity—which can easily be made from wind, the Sun, or hydropower—not plants, animal meat, or even Red Bull.

But wild transhumanist ambitions aside, my guess is most people won't be ready to upload their minds into machines at least for another few decades. However, with CRISPR gene editing tech, there are already DIY biohackers trying to splice plant DNA into their bodies so they can photosynthesize energy from the Sun. Of course, whoever figures this out will surely win the Nobel Prize, since they will also be potentially solving world hunger—and possibly saving the over 8000 kids that die globally from starvation or malnutrition every day.

My guess is that scientists will figure out some form of combining photosynthesis with human biology within a decade. And within two decades, it will become something pragmatic that can supplement our food intake—a so-called free lunch by just hanging out in the Sun.

Despite these two decent options, my money is on a third option—the brain implant that tells us we're satiated, even when our bodies are calorie restricted and yearning for food. Some studies suggest that maximum human longevity is best accomplished by minorly starving ourselves. If this is correct, it might be the best of both worlds, where humans eat dramatically less, but always feel like they're tummies are full because an implant stimulating our brain makes us feel it. If we take this one step further, maybe we can have our implants make us feel like we've just had a huge steak dinner, all the while knowing that cows haven't been eaten or cruelly slaughtered.

As a US presidential candidate, the reason I'm writing about veganism is I think it's a great movement (and there's a #VeganChalkChallenge catching on right now that is fun and I saw in my hometown Mill Valley, California). My love of animals runs deep, and whenever possible, I try not to eat meat myself—mainly because I don't want to hurt animals or be responsible for their deaths.

In the past, I've been on the front lines of the animal rights and preservation movement. For nearly two years, I was a director at a major wildlife organization called WildAid. I worked mostly in Southeast Asia, and our main goal was to stop illegal wildlife poaching. Before that, I was at National Geographic Channel, and in the field I wrote and filmed stories trying to raise awareness for a number of endangered animals.

I want veganism is to win its crusade. And in my opinion, the best way to tackle the crisis of harming animals is precisely how the driverless car manufacturers are treating one of world's greatest problems: drunk driving. Electric car manufacturers are not asking people to drink less—they are asking them not to drive at all. I think vegans should take a close look at transhumanism and ask if maybe—in 25 years or so—billions of animals around the world will have far better and longer lives because human appetite and eating have literally disappeared.

****

36) The Future of the LGBT Movement May Involve Transhumanism

The other night my wife and I were reading to our 4-year-old daughter a children's book that we borrowed from the public library. We came to a section where two characters — both who were the same sex — began having romantic feelings for each other. My wife and I smiled — we have many good LGBT friends.

Later that evening after putting my daughter to bed, I began wondering about the future of the LGBT movement, especially after Tim Cook, Apple's CEO and probably the world's most influential technologist, recently said he was proud to be gay. It's certainly interesting to speculate on how sexuality, sexual orientation, and society's interpretation of it all will change over the next 25 years as we charge headlong into the transhumanist age.

It shouldn't come as a surprise to anyone that the LGBT movement and transhumanism have a lot in common. Nearly all transhumanists support the LGBT cause. After all, a desire to be free to alter, express, and control one's sexual preference and identity sounds like a transhumanist concept. Advocates of transhumanism aim to alter, express, and control their bodies and preferences too, except they emphasize doing it with science and technology. If you look closely, the two movements — especially some of their major philosophies — are practically different sides of the same coin, and each is poised to gain strength from one another in the future as radical technologies transform the species.

In the next 25 years, the human being will undergo a larger transformation of its evolutionary body than it has undergone in the last 100,000 years. Artificial hearts will likely become better than real hearts. Telepathy via brain implants will become an important form of communication. Men will be able to give birth with implanted uteri. Each of these technologies already exists in some form and will soon be more widely available.

The million dollar question regarding these technologies is whether we will be allowed to freely use them. After all, the United States Congress is basically made up of all religious politicians, some whose faiths derive from texts that forbid anything like LGBT practices or transhumanism. Transhumanist's main goals are to overcome mortality and become as free and powerful as possible using technology—in essence, to become godlike.

For ages now, society has largely been afraid of transformation, especially when it concerns the human body or sexuality. Even today, a dozen U.S. states still have anti-sodomy laws, and LGBT people are often killed in places around the world — sometimes stoned to death — for their actions and beliefs. While victories have been won in the 21st century, such as in California and other states where people of the same sex can now officially marry, massive inequalities and bigotry still exist.

In the future, transhumanist technology and science will compliment the LGBT movement and help push it forward in the face of continued social oppression and closed-mindedness. This is important, since LGBT people are devoted to freedom. They want to be free to do anything they please without condemnation so long as it doesn't hurt others. Transhumanists — a notable number who are LGBT themselves — want the same exact thing. And they can work together to better achieve their goals.

With the onslaught of new tech and advanced medical and surgical techniques hitting the market, it's likely the LGBT movement will involve more transhumanist issues in the future. For those who are conservative and resist change, this may prove challenging. Take cybersex and virtual reality, for example, where Facebook's Oculus Rift and haptic suits will allow people from all corners of the world to have group sex if they want. Or what about fembots and sexbots, which already represent a growing 100 million dollar market? In 10 years, some robots may be as sophisticated as humans. Do we give them rights? Can we marry them? What if they're gay? What if we program them to not know if they're gay or not?

"The world is shifting under our feet," says B.J. Murphy, a pansexual transhumanist, writer, and futurist. "In 15 years, conservatives and anti-gay people will look back at the LGBT movement and yearn for an adversary so simple in its demands."

B.J. Murphy is right. The future will be anything but simple. Already, within two decade's time, parents may choose to have designer babies without certain sexual organs. Is a uterus necessary if you have ectogenesis (use of artificial wombs)? Or does it just present extra cancer risk and, for some, decades of painful, crampy menstrual cycles? Alternatively, will some religions encourage some males to be born with genetically lowered sex drives so they may have a better chance at becoming celibate priests, a shrinking vocation in the U.S.? Finally, will some seemingly narcissistic people procreate only through cloning techniques? The bizarre questions of the transhumanist age seem endless — and they are already being asked by a growing number of people.

Frankly, I could see many humans in the future stopping physical sex altogether as cranial implant technology finds precisely the right means to stimulate erogenous zones in the brain — something researchers are already working on. Real sex will probably not be able to match direct and scientifically targeted stimulation of our minds. Such actions may lead to a society where male and female traits disappear as pleasure becomes "on-demand," and gene therapy is able to combine the most functional parts of both genders into one entity. Not surprisingly, some institutions like marriage may end up going the way of the dinosaurs.

The LGBT movement has found firm footing in the 21st century — a testament to the courage of its supporters. I applaud them and support their courageous efforts. As a transhumanist, agnostic, and a politician, I stand ready to defend their freedoms and push their agenda forward, all the while knowing that the future will bring its own set of new challenges that none of us can easily foresee. In fact, the clash of civil rights in the transhumanist era may just be starting in a whole new way. Personhood, sexual freedom (virtual or not), and gender identity (or non-identity) will soon take on unprecedented roles in society, spurred by radical innovation and changing stereotypes of what it means to be a human being. For me, the wildcard of the future is not in society, but in the transformative technology that we invent and embrace.

****

37) An AI Global Arms Race is Looming

Forget about superintelligent AIs being created by a company, university, or a rogue programmer with Einstein-like IQ. Hollywood and its AI-themed movies like *Transcendence* and *Her* have misled the public. The launch of the first truly autonomous, self-aware artificial intelligence—one that has the potential to become far smarter than human beings—is a matter of the highest national and global security. Its creation could change the landscape of international politics in a matter of weeks—maybe even days, depending on how fast the intelligence learns to upgrade itself, hack and rewrite the world's best codes, and utilize weaponry.

In the last year, a chorus of leading technology experts, like Elon Musk, Stephen Hawking, and Bill Gates, have chimed in on the dangers regarding the creation of AI. The idea of a superintelligence on Planet Earth dwarfing the capacity of our own brains is daunting. Will this creation like its creators? Will it embrace human morals? Will it become religious? Will it be peaceful or warlike? The questions are innumerable and the answers are all debatable, but one thing is for sure from a national security perspective: If it's smarter than us, we want it to be on our side—the human race's side.

Now take that one step further, and I'm certain another theme regarding AI is just about to emerge—one bound with nationalistic fervor and patriotism. Politicians and military commanders around the world will want this superintelligent machine-mind for their countries and defensive forces. And they'll want it exclusively. Using AI's potential power and might for national security strategy is more than obvious—it's essential to retain leadership in the future world. Inevitably, a worldwide AI arms race is set to begin.

As the 2016 US Presidential candidate for the Transhumanist Party, I don't mind going out on a limb and saying the obvious: I also want AI to belong exclusively to America. Of course, I would hope to share the nonmilitary benefits and wisdom of a superintelligence with the world, as America has done for much of the last century with its groundbreaking innovation and technology. But can you imagine for a moment if AI was developed and launched in, let's say, North

Korea, or Iran, or increasingly authoritarian Russia? What if another national power told that superintelligence to break all the secret codes and classified material that America's CIA and NSA use for national security? What if this superintelligence was told to hack into the mainframe computers tied to nuclear warheads, drones, and other dangerous weaponry? What if that superintelligence was told to override all traffic lights, power grids, and water treatment plants in Europe? Or Asia? Or everywhere in the world except for its own country? The possible danger is overwhelming.

Below is something simple I've designed that's tautological in nature called the "AI Imperative." It demonstrates why an AI arms race is likely in humanity's future:

1) According to experts, a superintelligent AI is likely possible to create, and with enough resources, could be developed in a short amount of time (such as in 10-20 years).

2) Assuming we can control this superintelligent AI, whoever launches it first will likely always have the strongest superintelligence indefinitely, since that AI can be programmed to undermine and control all other AIs—if it allows any others to develop at all. Being first is everything in the superintelligent AI creation game (imagine if you were first to develop the Atomic bomb, and then also had the power to limit who else could ever develop one).

3) Whichever government launches and controls a superintelligent AI first will almost certainly end up the most powerful nation in the world because of it.

Given the AI Imperative, there's really only two likely courses of action for the world, even though there's four major possibilities on how to proceed. The first is to make AI development illegal all around the world—similar to chemical weapon development. However, people and companies probably would not go for it. We are a capitalistic civilization and the humanitarian benefits of AI are too promising to not create it. Stopping development of technology has never really worked, either. Someone else just ends up eventually doing it—either openly or in secret—if there's gain or profit to be made.

The other option is to be the first to create the superintelligent AI. That's the one my money is on—the one America is going to pick, regardless which political party is in office. America's military will likely spend as much of its resources as it needs to make sure it has exclusivity or majority control in the launch of a superintelligent AI. I'm guessing that trillions of dollars will be spent on AI development by the American military over the next ten years, regardless of national debt, economic conditions, or public disagreement. I'm betting that engineers, coders, and even hackers will become the new face of the American military, too. Our new warriors will be geeks working around the clock in the highest security environment possible. Think the Manhattan Project, but many more times in size and complexity.

Of course a third option is that AI is developed via a broad international consortium. However, nuclear weapon proliferation shows why, at least so far, this idea will likely not come to pass—at least on a worldwide level. As long as powerful nations like Russia and China independently push their flavor of social policy, economic development, and government operations (many of which largely mirror their leader's desires), this is unlikely to work or be accepted. This is because we're not talking about good old fashioned teamwork exploring outer space together on the space station or stopping developing-world civil wars and genocides, as the respected United Nations sometimes is involved in. We're talking about military power and protection of our families, citizenry, and livelihoods. There's much less room for cooperation when it concerns such personal matters.

A fourth option, one that I believe may be inevitable in the long run, is that all nations unite democratically and politically under one flag, one elected leadership, and one government, in an effort to better control the technology that is ushering in the transhumanist age—such as superintelligent AI. Then, all together, we create this intelligence. I like the sound of this from a philosophical and humanitarian point of view. The problem with it is such a plan takes time and many proud people to swallow their egos and cultural differences—and with only about 10 to 20 years before superintellitent AI is created, no one is going to push hard for that option.

So, inevitably, we are back to our looming dog-eat-dog AI arms race. It may not be one filled with nuclear fallout shelters like yesteryear, but it will show all the signs of the most powerful nations and the best minds they posses vying against one another for an all-important future national security. More importantly, it's a winner-takes-all scenario. The competition of the century is set to begin.

****

38) Will Transhumanism Change Racism in the Future?

Despite decades of progress, racism and bigotry are still prevalent in the United States. Often, they even dominate the news in American media, like during the Baltimore riots or the Ferguson shooting. Movements like Black Lives Matter remind us that the society we live in still has many biases to be fought against, but that good work can be done to combat bigotry if people unite against it.

Despite this, the quest to find true equality in the world is about to get more complicated. It's possible the ability to completely change skin color may arrive in the next 15-30 years. Like a chameleon, expect humans to literally change their skin color soon through coming technologies—most that will probably be based on genetic editing.

Already, humans have the technology to change the color of eyes and choose the sex of their offspring. But on the horizon are new techniques—based on CRISPR genetic editing technology—that may permanently or temporarily alter the melanin in our skin (the pigment mostly responsible for its color). And like some characters in the X-Men film series, we may even be able to do this in real-time someday.

Transhumanists with Do-It-Yourself CRISPR kits are already experimenting with the technology. But few formal scientists have dared to question how and if CRISPR may change race issues in the future.

In a conversation with CBS News, Dr. Arthur Caplan, founding director of the division of medical ethics at NYU Langone Medical Center's Department of Population Health, evaded the question:

CBS News asked: *Does that mean scientists will be able to engineer changes to eye or skin color, or give people mega-strength?*

Maybe, said Caplan. "I think it's reasonable to presume you could tweak things for strength, more muscles, endurance, or to be able to run or travel further." You might be able to enhance memory, to make a person able to retain more or learn faster, he said.

Someday, he said, "I think you could tweak genes that would allow you to perceive more. You might be able to see more like a bat, sense more of the radiation spectrum. See ultraviolet light and parts of the energy spectrum we don't see but that other creatures do. Eagle-eye vision."

"You could certainly make people more disease resistant, less likely to get a cold or the flu. Or to fight off MRSA or E. coli — build up their immune systems. Enhance them so they could enjoy more pleasure. They've been doing a teeny, tiny bit in animals," said Caplan, who will lead sessions on ethical and regulatory issues of gene editing in animal research next week in Washington, DC.

I don't blame Caplan for not answering the loaded part of the question from CBS. It's a thorny subject to think that a technology we already have in our hands can literally change the very physicality of our beings.

Of course, it's not just changing skin color that's controversial. There are transhumanists who want to grow tails, horns, and even fish gills so they can breathe underwater. And some are already trying to do it. My favorite experiment of transhumanists is the attempt to create photosynthesis capabilities in their bodies—in an effort to feed themselves for free and end world hunger by getting energy directly from the sun.

These new citizen scientist experiments go under the banner of biohacking—and it's quickly become one of the fastest growing aspects of transhumanism. Many biohackers are millennials and aiming to revolutionize what it means to be human.

Biohackers also make me think of the original *Star Wars* movie where Luke Skywalker first meets Hans Solo amongst a plethora of strange-looking creatures in a rough bar on planet Tatooine. Such a scene in real life is no longer just possible, but likely now given CRISPR technology.

I'm guessing that genetic editing techniques and bionic fabrication will allow us to do things to our bodies we never thought possible. In fact, with the growing of neuro-technology advances, there is now even talk of adding a third eye on the back of the head in biohacker communities. Some blind people have robotic eyes that already enable them to see.

If you're asking yourself if this is all ethical, the real question is: Why isn't it ethical? Transhumanists believe we should be able to do anything we want with our bodies so long as it's not hurting others, a staple of the newly written *Transhumanist Bill of Rights*.

Bear in mind ideas like this have long been underway already. For example, transgender surgery has become more common. And 3D printed body parts also are being used to help people in need. And many older persons are already a cyborg in some way or another, having artificial hips, dentures, or something else synthetic in them. I have a RFID chip in my hand that allows me to start a car without keys.

All these technologies and advances aside, the Tatooine bar in *Star Wars* highlights another aspect of future racism—that of droids versus biological creatures. In the bar, the bartender—upon seeing Luke Skywalker with C-3PO and R2-D2—shouts: "We don't serve their kind here."

Robots are just about to make their entrance into the world in a big way, occupying households, helping with chores, and teaching our kids mathematics. In fact, on my cross country presidential campaign bus tour, I traveled with a 4-foot robot onboard. Everyone loved the machine, but if they had known it was videoing everything, would they still be as enthused?

Some of these issues were brought up recently with Google Glass, where resistance was met with the technology in public. I also own this device. People always give me strange, cynical looks, especially if I wear my Google Glass into a restaurant or at a non-tech conference.

Of course, racism has one more major new arena of technology to contend with—that of the virtual world. Avatars can basically be designed to appear in any way someone wants. So people can represent themselves to others in totally different ways. Some might say the avatar is a costume, but early reports of virtual hate and rape online have shown that people (mainly their feelings but sometimes their bodies as in the case of a hacked Vibease vibrator) can indeed be hurt, and such a thing can even have legal consequence.

Through the use of new technologies, society will have to grapple with continued forms of bigotry in the everchanging landscape of being human. But skin color may soon not be the dominant theme of racism, but rather the choice of what appearance we choose to reveal ourselves. I hope the diversity that technology gives us on who to be will make us far more accepting of each other and our multitude of personalities and behaviors.

****

CHAPTER VII: HOW WEIRD CAN THE FUTURE GET?

39) Let's Cure the Disease of Sleeping

To me, sleeping is a disease. Luckily, in the next 25 years, scientists may cure it. For millions, that cure can't come soon enough. I hate sleeping and always have. I see sleeping as an early form of dipping in and out of death. Sleeping is probably the most wasteful thing all humans do—we spend a third of our lives in basically a lobotomized state. I wish I could I will myself from doing it, but like everyone else, I'm a slave to my body and mind, and I require sleep to function normally.

In my 20s, while sailing across the oceans and being a journalist, I tried everything to not sleep. I chugged coffee and popped NoDoz (caffeine pills) daily, sometimes up to five tablets a day. For a year, I fought to keep my sleeping to about four and a half hours a night. Unfortunately, that was just not enough for my body and mind to be at its sharpest. And over time, caffeine just simply didn't wake me up anymore. To stay up and write my articles coherently, I'd often pull the hair on my arms until the pain was severe enough it jolted my brain to attention.

Currently, I live in San Francisco and hang out with a lot of busy Silicon Valley types. Some friends—often CEOs—claim to only sleep three to four hours a night. I get jealous when I hear that. But, of course, that's partially why they're generally so successful. They have more time to work instead of counting sheep. Even the recent Wall Street sequel was titled *Money Never Sleeps*.

Like everyone who hates sleep, there are ways to make the best of a bad situation. To make sleeping more worthwhile, I read a few books on how to dream better and how best to record my thoughts after I awoke (with a journal on my nightstand). Indeed, some great ideas and art in the world have come about as a result of dreams. And I tend to dream big, especially when I do certain wacky drugs or eat heavy foods before bed. The problem is that while dreams on occasion do give me interesting ideas, it's only while awake that I analytically consider them and possibly find use for them. And I always feel I could've just thought them up while awake if I wanted to, anyway. Besides, mostly my dreams are a mosh pit of craziness stemming from the so-called alligators in my mind. Rarely are they pleasant.

Another pastime I took up was lucid dreaming. I did learn how to fly on demand, dream in vivid colors, and control to some extent what I wanted to do, not unlike Neo in *The Matrix*. The problem is, lucid dreaming is a major hassle to accomplish—it requires concentration before you go to bed, and concentration while sleeping. Hence, it doesn't feel like sleep at all, and therefore isn't very rejuvenative.

While much has been made about how beneficial a good night of sleep is, few discuss that sleeping is stealing away conscious time with loved ones, hampering economies around the world, and even indirectly hurting our bodies. We should never forget we age whether we're awake or sleeping. And while the studies say the better we sleep the longer we live, this information may be misleading. I believe we age much more in our sleep than our lifespans gain from sleeping well. Sleeping—like being awake—is slowly killing us.

Scientifically speaking, sleep is a process where internal restoration and recuperation of the body and mind takes place. Sleep is comprised of various cycles, which are often separated by two classifications: non-REM and REM sleep.

There are numerous researchers in the world working on ways to try to remain alert despite sleep deprivation. One well-known study seemed to herald a breakthrough when it showed a natural occurring brain hormone Orexin-A that reversed the effects of sleepiness in monkeys.

Unfortunately, it appears most studies on sleep are being done to treat insomnia and other chronic sleeping disorders, which affect approximately 40 million people in America. That's why I like some of the military studies on sleep deprivation better. They are not only after curing sleeping disorders, but getting their troops to stay awake longer and with more focus.

One of the more promising techniques being experimented with is transcranial direct-current stimulation (tDCS), where an alternating current is administered to the dorsolateral prefrontal cortex. As Jessa Gamble reports in *Aeon*, "tDCS uses a very mild charge, not enough directly to cause neurons to fire, but just enough to slightly change their polarization, lowering the threshold at which they do so."

After short 30 minutes sessions of this tDCS treatment, patients are reputed to be more awake and able to learn better. They also can sleep less and sleep better.

Other methods of sleeping less—including those of biohackers—involve sleeping better and getting to sleep quicker. Bulletproof's Dave Asprey suggests taking a blend of amino acids, magnesium, and potassium before bed. He also says do breathing exercises before bed, don't drink coffee after 2 PM, and try to sleep in total darkness. For some people, Asprey also suggests a CES (cranial electrotherapy stimulation) machine to run a current across the brain at between 0.5 and 1.5hz (the range of physical regenerative sleep). One of the most well-known ones is the FDA-cleared Fisher Wallace Stimulator.

For now, those like myself who don't like to sleep will have to use a combination of science, diet, technology, and stimulants to have more waking hours of the day. But hopefully in the near future scientists will invent a way to avoid sleep altogether. My guess is in the next 15 to 25 years a cranial implant that directly stimulates focusing and thinking powers in the brain—perhaps building upon tDCS technology—will at least get us to a point where we don't need more than two hours of sleep a night. Two hours lost, I can handle. But sleeping a third of my life away—or approximately 26 years on average—is not only insane, but tragic.

****

40) When Computers Insist They Are Alive

Ever since college, where I focused some of my studies on the strange topic of a brain in a vat, it's troubled me that some people think only humans are capable of consciousness—rationally knowing what they are and that they exist.

Such biased thinking smells of anthropomorphic prejudice. Machines can be just as aware of their own consciousness as people, and perhaps more so, if they're programmed that way.

While the three-pound brain and its hundred billion neurons remain the least understood organ of the human body, most experts agree on a standard explanation: Human consciousness is a compilation of many chemicals in the brain forced through a prism that produces cognitive awareness designed to insist an entity is aware of not only itself but also the outside world. As an atheist and science-minded person, I buy this simplistic meat bag explanation.

But there's probably a lot more to consciousness, especially if we consider the future of superintelligence consciousnesses. To understand it and the field that encapsulates it—epistemology, the study of knowledge, with a special emphasis on what can be proven and what can't—it's always useful to start with French philosopher and mathematician Rene Descartes. He may have made the initial step by saying I think, therefore I am. But thinking does not adequately define consciousness. Justifying thinking is much closer to the meaning that's adequate. It really should be: I believe I'm conscious, therefore I am.

Delving further into this point, some computers can already think on various rudimentary levels, but we do not say they are conscious because they don't insist they are conscious. If they did, then many would argue we are dealing with a bonafide life form. However, no experts argue such a thing, at least not yet.

The recent near-future sci-fi movie *Ex Machina* highlights some of the core dilemmas between whether a machine intelligence is alive and truly conscious, or whether it's just following its circuitry. The story follows a human and an AI robot getting to know one another. One can't watch it and not think about the ongoing nature versus nurture controversy—the millennia-old debate of how and why humans acquired their behavior. It's this egocentric behavior that makes most humans justify their own conscious identity.

However, philosophically, *Ex Machina* also challenges us to ask another critical question about consciousness: What part does free will play in consciousness, if any at all? It's an interesting question, but in my opinion, the more poignant inquiry is not whether conscious entities, like humans, have free will, but whether there could ever be a consciousness without free will. Anomalies, randomness, and potentially even built-in chaos seemingly must remain intrinsic parts of the picture—otherwise it's all deterministic.

Some fictional computers, such as HAL in Stanley Kubrick's classic *2001: A Space Odyssey*, have insisted they were alive and fully conscious. And indeed, HAL appeared to be so. What made HAL conscious and alive to us, rather than some awkward Honda robot or IBM's chess champion Deep Blue, was that HAL had his own set of desires, demands, and identity. Because of this, there's no question HAL would pass the Turing Test—a test where a robot attempts to pass for being a human, something no machine has truly successful accomplished yet in the 21st century.

Some machine intelligent experts swear by the Turing Test. But is it the all-important test we make it out to be in determining intelligence and consciousness? If we met a far more advanced being—maybe a superintelligence from the future—what would their test of us be called? Would they say we have a lower form of consciousness than they do? Would they even say we have a consciousness at all?

Probably not. After all, what human believes a fish has a consciousness? Or a seagull? Or even a dog? Consciousness is built upon massive complexity—and the power to make sense of and identify oneself upon that complexity. Anthropomorphizing everything is part of that conscious process, as egotistical as that sounds. Our consciousness is specifically built upon the ability to know we have the power to craft our own destiny amongst the material world around us.

So what test might a superintelligence give us to see if we possess a so-called consciousness comparable to their own? To even tackle that question, we first have to answer if there's something outside of free will that reflects a higher consciousness

I think consciousness, as we know it, isn't dependent on free will. A significantly smarter intelligence than us could be completely run on wiring with no free will at all, and it would still appear far freer, abler, more creative, and more alive than us in its decisions and actions. Consciousness is therefore relative, at least to humans.

Perhaps, then, the real test a superintelligence would give us would not be based on any notion of free will or justification of consciousness, but upon the basis for complexity and the speed to successfully navigate that complexity. That certainly sounds like a machine-like thing to do. But I think there's more to it, as well. I think a superintelligence's test of humans would also involve the ability to transcend mammalian limitations and biases—something I refer to as *artificial intelligence relativism*. Good and evil, and morality as a whole—except for being functional—would have to be checked at the door.

I've questioned in my writings before that the critical component of a superintelligence's morality is that there is none, at least nothing human-like. Morality in a machine, or in a deterministic consciousness, is nothing more than mathematical algorithm of rule-bound precision. This leaves little room for humanity and love for another, or any of the mammalian niceties that people swear by. It seems, then, that the Turing Test for superintelligence is to deny the lack of notable value for anything outside oneself. Pure narcissism, mixed with nearly unlimited computational power, is therefore the quintessential part of a test of what comprises a superintelligent consciousness.

****

41) The Drug Lords of Tomorrow Will be Biohackers

Through various sources—mainly transhumanist biohacker friends—I've been hearing about how some drug traffickers might be taking an interest in brain implant technology.

If scientists can get a brain implant to give neural stimuli that affects our perspectives, moods, and behaviors, then the future of drugs could be totally different than what it is now. In fact, in such a future, drug creation would become the domain of engineers and coders. This could become the next major frontier of the so-called drug market.

About half a million people already have chips connected to their brains. Most of these are cochlear implants to aid against deafness, but some are also deep brain stimulation (DBS) types, sometimes used for Alzheimer's, Parkinson's disease, and epilepsy.

Generally speaking, DBS cranial implants work by firing electrical impulses via electrodes into certain regions of the brain. In the case of epileptic patients, they help control seizures.

But improving forms of brain implants may use more EEG technology—a part of the brain-computer interface field—where they can distribute brain waves over a certain portion of the brain. If this portion is one that affects mood—thought to be determined mostly by the amygdala—maybe they'll be able to give us a real high.

Thync is already an external device claiming to work something like this. Only out this year, wearers have been reporting some success with the device, which can give you a quick electronic pick-up or help you achieve inner calm. And the gadget looks cool too.

Of course, the holy grail of brain implants would be the sex chip. A physician has experimented with this before, working on directly stimulating the erogenous zones of the brain. The researcher was reported to be seeking investments to make the implant commercially affordable.

If a wealthy drug lord were to get this type of technology and further develop it, they might sell time slots of stimulation to people who received the implants. For example, you might use your smartphone to purchase an hour of sexual ecstasy.

Of course, this might also be accomplished simply by a brainwave headset, but I think it's the chip implant will really take off. After all, if you're at work or at home with your spouse, you might not want them to know you're walking around with a digital high all day or being sexually stimulated. So the privacy of implants may make headsets obsolete someday.

A big benefit of implants too might be how it deals with addicts. Perhaps if a user has addiction problems, the chip could be used to wean themselves of the drug, or only allow certain amounts—ones that never allow the user to miss work, or become violent, or anything that disrupts one's lifestyle too much.

Fundamentally, the reason implants will probably be the "drug" of choice over plant or chemical substances is because of this type of possible perfect control. One could program it so chips could never overdose people—whereas a problem people always have with drugs is quality. People never really know what they're getting until after they've taken it—and then they can't stop it. With plants or something made in an illegal laboratory like LSD, it's always a crapshoot to know what you're getting, the quality of it, and especially where it came from. With chips and downloads, there would always be a digital trail and signal to follow.

One major challenge with cranial implant highs is hacking. How can you avoid hackers messing with programming? A bad trip could be really bad. But here again, perhaps a foolproof program could make it so a chip could never harm an individual, and would shut down automatically and immediately if it ever did. And of course users might be able to control their implant stimuli by their smartphones or other devices.

Obviously, such dangers will be the focus of big government too. Probably like many recreational drugs, the most important question is whether government would allow brain implants for recreational uses at all. However, if they don't, and brain implant technology keeps developing, maybe in a few decades the War on Drugs will soon involve a War on Implants.

I've tried most every drug I know—and cautiously support legalization of all drugs—and I would enjoy having the freedom to experiment with brain chips and the kind of new experiences they might offer.

Naturally, illegal drug suppliers will be interested in this coming transhumanist field of implants and direct brain stimuli—and may play a big part in it, especially if government outlaws it as dangerous (which they probably will, at least at first). However the future of cranial implants unfolds, I hope the public will welcome new experiences through technology that safely allow us to expand our minds.

****

42) Should I Have Had My Cat Cryonically Preserved?

I recently made the agonizing decision to euthanize my cat Ollie, who I adopted 13 years before from the streets.

Ollie had barely eaten or drank anything for five days and was dying from kidney failure. The veterinarian told me Ollie would probably be dead in 24 hours and suggested euthanizing him, so that his death wasn't caused by choking or something horrible like that when other organs failed. I reluctantly agreed.

Pet euthanasia generally includes a heavy morphine-based sedative that peacefully knocks the animal out, followed by a heart stopper-chemical injection. We euthanized Ollie on his favorite couch in my home. While the process seemed painless and quick, it was absolutely heartbreaking for my family and me.

Days after the death, a number of transhumanist friends consoled me and told me of their own dealings with pet deaths. Since I'm a life extension advocate, I'm well-versed in procedures for dealing with (and avoiding) human death. But I didn't really know much about pets.

It turns out many transhumanists have already thought of these and some have even undergone cryonic procedures with their animals—the process where they cryogenically freeze their pets in hopes to resurrect them in the future when the technology becomes available. The Michigan-based Cryonics Institute has 120 frozen pets.

Christine Gaspar, a nurse and longtime cryonicist, is one friend who did this. She froze her cat at the Cryonics Institute, and the process cost her about $5,700, she told me.

I thought deeply about doing this with Ollie, but decided against it for a few reasons—reasons I hope I won't later regret in my life as the world and technology rapidly advances.

To begin with, I was a little late in the process with Ollie. It was already 24 hours after he died that I began considering cryonics for him, and, like humans, the cryonics process works best if it's begun within hours of death—especially to preserve the brain and its memories. Also, $5,700 is quite a chunk of cash—plus there are yearly maintenance costs. Additionally, my kids are already yearning for another pet, and my parents have had seven different pets so far in their lives.

With this mind, I even considered the cheaper preservation methods, where a bucket filled with formaldehyde, glutereldahyde, or some other solution is used to preserve the pet. Then one can just keep the body in their garage. In this procedure, at least much of the tissue, bones, and organs might be able to be salvaged in the future when trying to reanimate the animal. Some people even stuff their pet or freeze-dry them to keep them in their house, looking as if they were almost alive.

In the end, I passed on all these options and opted for a normal burial of Ollie in my backyard, which my young daughters and wife attended.

The truth is I tend to believe I'll be merged with AI in about 30-40 years—and soon entering the Singularity afterward—so the idea of loving a cat indefinitely seemed less tangible.

I also wondered if in the future, we'd be able—and maybe even obligated—to make our pets hyper-intelligent via cranial implant technology and radical genetics. Then the animal, like an adult offspring, becomes intelligent enough to make its own decisions. What if Ollie didn't want to live? Or be so intelligent? Or even be my pet anymore? What if Ollie became smarter than me through radical tech and upgrades he acquired without my permission (and I became his pet)? Such is the weird world of transhumanist thinking—and the future many of us will face in the coming decades.

Either way, Ollie's death started me down exploring the road of technology and science we are going to impose on the creatures we love. It turns out the pet industry is exploding with transhuman—or if you will, transanimal—themes. Most of these have nothing to do with death, but instead have to do with giving animals a better life so humans can enjoy them more.

For starters, an entire cottage industry on pet-tech wearables has emerged, with numerous start-ups already competing in the space. *Motherboard* reported there will likely be exhibition space specifically dedicated at CES 2017 to pet tech. Currently, the leading wearables are Fitbit-like devices that help monitor dogs' whereabouts and health.

Of course, pets have long had RFID chip implants to help locate them, and their success has led the way of implants into humans—such as the one I now have in my hand. But the future of tech for pets is also developing too. There are devices like TailTalk and the KYON collar that can supposedly tell you about your animal's mood. Some companies have even launched projects to try to directly read the brain waves of pets, so one day you might be able to discuss Plato's Allegory of a Cave—or the adventures of Garfield.

As cool as some of the tech coming out for pets is, the world is headed for a massive transformation about how and what it wants in its future pets. CRISPR gene editing is already here, and the idea of creating a pet dinosaur is no longer a pipe dream. In fact, *MIT Technology Review* reports that Chinese scientists have already created "designer pets."

It's possible in just a few years' time we will be creating new creatures that contain the very best elements pets have. Shed-less dogs. Uber-cuddly cats. Melodic singing songbirds. Why not combine them? Why not add some reptilian genes too, for excitement? In fact, why not just make a make a mini-Brontosaurus?

Of course, the other type of future pet will be created by secretive company Magic Leap, where sensors on your ceiling can put out a holographic pet image that you can interact with and order around.

Why not have an eight-foot tall Tyrannosaurs Rex inside to scare off burglars when they break in? Or a 30-foot anaconda? Or a pack of wolves? Best yet, you can program the holographic wolves to take turns reading your toddlers *The Three Little Pigs*.

The future of transhuman pets, though, is not holographic or biological. It's robotic. The field of robotic dogs already available on the market is massive. There are a few dozen companies and types of robotic dogs out there. Some of these machines are designed to be legitimate guard dogs, and can offer real security via movement tracking mechanisms and security software. In the near future, some will offer Skype abilities, so you can see through cameras in their eyes what's happening in your house—like if your child is playing with the stove. Other robot dogs will have built in fire alarms that can register smoke in a child's room or spot a poisonous spider in the dark crawling on a bed crib.

In about five years, robot dogs will be so sophisticated they will walk our children to school, carry our groceries for us from the car, and probably even have built in drone capabilities to fly. We'll program them to catch rats but not fight with the neighbor's cat. They won't need to be fed, they'll know how to recharge themselves, and gone forever will be the days of shoveling dog poo. And of course, they'll easily beat us in chess.

Some new pet robots have fake fur too. In the future, we can expect robotic pets to have non-shedding, clean smelling fur that is dirt resistant and looks just like a real pet. And the pet's bodies will be soft and padded, with heat creating capabilities to keep you warm at night when it sleeps with you.

Like so many other things technology is changing for the human race, the central role pets play in our lives will also change. The domestication of animals has evolved for thousands of years, but the next 25 years may end pet relationships as we know them. While I'm still a little unsure whether I should've cryo-preserved my cat, I think Ollie would've found it strange to be brought back to a world with chess-playing robot dogs, holographic wolves in the living room, and mini-Tyrannosaurus Rexs cruising around the backyard.

****

43) The Language of Aliens Will Always be Indecipherable

There's about 170 billion galaxies in the observable universe—and as the technology of our telescopes improves, humans will probably discover as many as a trillion galaxies. Galaxies, like our own, can contain 200 billion or more planets and stars. Inevitably, some of those celestial worlds are capable of bringing forth and nurturing intelligent life. In fact, to some top astronomers, the question is not whether aliens exist, but how many millions of different intelligent extraterrestrial species exist.

With so many possible advanced life forms out there, the obvious question is: Why haven't humans made contact with them yet? This famous conundrum is called the Fermi Paradox.

There are at least a dozen cogent answers to the Fermi Paradox, but only a few delve into the communication of extraterrestrial civilizations—something which must exist in some form for us to even know about them. And none of the answers about communication adequately discuss what happens to alien language in an accelerating intelligence explosion, which is what must happen for them to be advanced enough to make contact with us.

Modern day humans—and presumably other advanced intelligent species—are generally in a state of exponential technological and evolutionary growth. That growth may not perfectly reflect Moore's Law (where microprocessor speeds double approximately every 24 months), but it's probably somewhere in the ballpark.

This technological growth leads to only one place: the Singularity, a state of existence that is so advanced humans can name it but not adequately describe it. It's a place that transcends the understanding our three-pound brains can muster—a place where progress in the last minute of existence might be more progress than all of history combined before it. And all smart aliens end up in the Singularity.

With this in mind, make sure not to imagine aliens as slimy green monsters portrayed in Hollywood films. An extraterrestrial species even 100 years more advanced than 21st century humans has likely discarded their biological bodies, deeming them unstable and too primitive. Instead, advanced aliens merged with machines and became data to serve their growing superintelligence needs.

After aliens are well into the Singularity, they probably discovered ways to influence and control individual atoms, thereby giving them the ability to merge and manifest as anything in the universe. So now they could be anywhere and everywhere. Some transhumanists call this phenomenon: Omnipotism.

But the key point here is that extra 100 years of evolutionary advancement. In our case, the end of that timeline from 2016 would put us in the early next century. I'll call it Jethro's Window, after the protagonist in my futurist novel The Transhumanist Wager, because there's a critical point in time from where we are as humans today (it starts with the invention of the microprocessor) to the point when we reach the Singularity.

Here's the sad solution to Fermi's Paradox: We've never discovered other life forms because language and communication methods in the Singularity evolve so rapidly that even in one minute, an entire civilization can become transformed and totally unintelligible. In an expanding universe that is at least 13.6 billion years old, this transformation might never end. What this means is we will never have more than a few seconds to understand or even notice our millions of neighbors. The nature of the universe—the nature of communication in a universe where intelligence exponentially grows—is to keep us forever unaware and alone.

The only time we may discover other intelligent life forms is that 100 or so years during Jethro's Window, and then it requires the miracle of another species in a similar evolutionary time table, right then, looking for us too. Given the universe is so gargantuan and many billions of years old, even with millions of alien species out there, we'll never find them. We'll never know them. It's an unfortunate mathematical certainty.

****

44) Liberty Might Be Better Served by Doing Away with Privacy

The constant onslaught of new technology is making our lives more public and trackable than ever, which understandably scares a lot of people. Part of the dilemma is how we interpret the right to privacy using centuries-old ideals handed down to us by our forbearers. I think the 21st century idea of privacy—like so many other taken-for-granted concepts—may need a revamp.

When James Madison wrote the Fourth Amendment—which helped legally establish US privacy ideals and protection from unreasonable search and seizure—he surely wasn't imagining Elon Musk's neural lace, artificial intelligence, the internet, or virtual reality. Madison wanted to make sure government couldn't antagonize its citizens and overstep its governmental authority, as monarchies and the Church had done for centuries in Europe.

For many decades, the Fourth Amendment has mostly done its job. But privacy concerns in the 21st century go way beyond search and seizure issues: Giant private companies like Google, Apple, and Facebook are changing our sense of privacy in ways the government never could. And many of us have plans to continue to use more new tech; one day, many of us will use neural prosthetics and brain implants. These brain-to-machine interfaces will likely eventually lead to the hive mind, where everyone can know each other's precise whereabouts and thoughts at all times, because we will all be connected to each other through the cloud. Privacy, broadly thought of as essential to a democratic society, might disappear.

"While privacy has long been considered a fundamental right, it has never been an inherent right," Jeremy Rifkin, an American economic and social theorist, wrote in *The Zero Marginal Cost Society*. "Indeed, for all of human history, until the modern era, life was lived more or less publicly, as befits most species on Earth."

The question of whether privacy needs to change is really a question of functionality. Is privacy actually useful for individuals or for society? Does having privacy make humanity better off? Does privacy raise the standard of living for the average person?

In some ways, these questions are futile. Technological innovation is already calling the shots, and considering the sheer amount of new tech being bought and used, most people seem content with the more public, transparent world it's ushering in. Hundreds of millions of people willingly use devices and tech that can monitor them, including personal home assistants, credit cards, smartphones, and even pacemakers (in Ohio, a suspect's own pacemaker data will be used in the trial against him.) Additionally, cameras in cities are ubiquitous; tens of thousands of fixed cameras are recording every second of the day, making a walk outside one's own home a trackable affair. Even my new car knows where I'm at and calls me on the car intercom if it feels it's been hit or something suspicious is happening.

Because of all this, in the not so distant future—perhaps as little as 15 years—I imagine a society where everybody can see generally where anyone else is at any moment. Many companies already have some of this ability through the tech we own, but it's not in the public's hands yet to control.

For many, this constant state of being monitored is concerning. But consider that much of our technology can also look right back into the government's world with our own spying devices and software. It turns out Big Brother isn't so big if you're able to track his every move.

The key with such a reality is to make sure government is engulfed by ubiquitous transparency too. Why shouldn't our government officials be required to be totally visible to us all, since they've chosen public careers? Why shouldn't we always know what a police officer is saying or doing, or be able to see not only when our elected Senator meets with lobbyists, but what they say to them?

For better or worse, we can already see the beginnings of an era of in which nothing is private: WikiLeaks has its own transparency problems and has a scattershot record of releasing documents that appear to be politically motivated, but nonetheless has exposed countless political emails, military wires, and intel documents that otherwise would have remained private or classified forever. There is an ongoing battle about whether police body camera footage should be public record. Politicians and police are being videotaped by civilians with cell phones, drones, and planes.

But it's not just government that's a worry. It's also important that people can track companies, like Google, Apple, and Facebook that create much of the software that tracks individuals and the public. This is easier said than done, but a vibrant start-up culture and open-source technology is the antidote. There will always be people and hackers that insist on tracking the trackers, and they will also lead the entrepreneurial crusade to keep big business in check with new ways of monitoring their behavior. There are people hacking and cracking big tech's products to see what their capabilities are and to uncover surreptitious surveillance and security vulnerabilities. This spirit must extend to monitoring all of big tech's activities. Massive openness must become a two-way street.

And I'm hopeful it will, if disappearing privacy trends continue their trajectory, and if technology continues to connect us omnipresently (remember the hive mind?). We will eventually come to a moment in which all communications and movements are public by default.

In such a world, everyone will be forced to be more honest, especially Washington. No more backdoor special interest groups feeding money to our lawmakers for favors. And there would be fewer incidents like Governor Chris Christie believing he can shut down public beaches and then use them himself without anyone finding out. The recent viral photo—taken by a plane overhead—of him bathing on a beach he personally closed is a strong example of why a non-private society has merit.

If no one can hide, then no one can do anything wrong without someone else knowing. That may allow a better, more efficient society with more liberties than the protection privacy accomplishes.

This type of future, whether through cameras, cell phone tracking, drones, implants, and a myriad of other tech could literally shape up America, quickly stopping much crime. Prisons would eventually likely mostly empty, and dangerous neighborhoods would clean up—instead of putting people in jail, we can track them with drones until their sentence is up. Our internet of things devices will call the cops when domestic violence disputes arrive (it was widely reported—but not confirmed—that a smarthome device called the police when a man was allegedly brandishing a gun and beating his girlfriend. Such cases will eventually become commonplace.)

A society lacking privacy would have plenty of liberty-creating phenomena too, likely ushering in an era similar to the 60s where experimental drugs, sex, and artistic creation thrived. Openness, like the vast internet itself, is a facilitator of freedom and personal liberties. A less private society means a more liberal one where unorthodox individuals and visionaries—all who can no longer be pushed behind closed doors—will be accepted for who or what they are.

Like the Heisenberg principle, observation changes reality. So does a lack of walls between you and others. A radical future like this would bring an era of freedom and responsibility back to humanity and the individual. We are approaching an era where the benefits of a society that is far more open and less private will lead to a safer, diverse, more empathetic world. We should be cautious, but not afraid.

****

45) Quantum Archaeology: The Quest to 3D Bioprint Every Dead Person Back to Life

My brother-in-law recently died after a brutal fight with cancer. At 48 years of age, he left behind two young children, a loving wife, and a thriving real estate business he built. After the funeral and burial of the body, I was given some of his best suits and jackets to wear. I took them, not only to use them, but possibly to give them back to him in the future.

As a secular transhumanist—someone who advocates for improving humanity by merging people with machines—I don't believe in death anymore. At least, I don't believe in biological death's permanency the way most people do. Most people think after death, the buried or cremated physical body decays into earth and stardust—the same stuff from which it originally came. They are correct.

But earth and stardust can also be forged, arranged, and ultimately 3D printed to create life. After all, humans and their brains are mostly just meat. What makes a human—and the three pounds of gray matter we all carry on our shoulders called a brain—be able to fly to the moon, play Mozart's 5th Symphony, and admire sunsets is how subatomic particles in that meat interact and play off each other. The jury is still out, but many futurists and technologists like me believe the subatomic world is just discernable math—a puzzle of numbers (and possibly some unpredictable variables) waiting to be calculated by super sophisticated microprocessors we will inevitably have in the next 30 or so years.

The quagmire here is if computers can one day calculate complete realities, including a specific moment in time of an entire physical human being, then all we have to do to resurrect the dead is to 3D print them out. Given that scientists are already having success 3D printing biological tissue, some people believe we'll be able to do this with the dead in less than 50 years. This mind-blowing field is called Quantum Archaeology.

Before we delve too far into real-time technological resurrection, it's important to understand the driving force behind such radical technology, as well as the anti-death landscape of the burgeoning transhumanist movement—a movement which leads the Quantum Archaeology charge. Most transhumanists #1 goal is to become immortal through science.

The history of transhumanism mirrors the history of the microprocessor. Quietly, behind the daily noise of Trumpian politics, bickering world religions, and dark environmental warnings, an unquestionable civilization-changing phenomenon is occurring: the 50-year old microprocessor continues to evolve exponentially. While the human brain approximately doubled in size over the last 2000,000 to 800,000 years, the microprocessor doubles its speed every 18-24. Some experts think in just 15 years' time, our smart phones will be more intelligent than us. In three decades time, they will almost certainly be hundreds of times smarter than us.

Transhumanists hope to merge themselves—both brains and bodies—with these super smart machines to both survive indefinitely and to thrive in the future world. In fact, if people don't merge with computers, humans may soon become an unintelligent species compared to the machine intelligence that will exist. But humans will directly merge with technology; Already, hundred-million dollar companies in California are working on neural prosthetics designed to connect our thoughts to computers. Various universities are working on robotic eyes to give us Superman vision that will also stream Netflix directly and social media into our optic nerve. Others, like myself, already have implants that can start cars, open doors, and pay for things. Some biohackers even want to cut off their limbs and replace them with robotic ones—synthetic body parts which in a decade's time may be better than our own biology. I believe the future is already set. Many humans will electively put significant tech in their bodies that make them more productive while also increasing their survivability.

When transhumanist friends hear of my brother-in-law's passing, they tell me how doubly tragic it is—given that humans stand a good chance to overcome the dilemma of aging, death, and disease in the next 25 years because of coming radical technology. Transhumanists consider this the most important period in human history—because if they can survive the next few decades, they will likely be able to survive forever with the help of science.

Along with various medical professionals, like leading gerontologist Dr. Aubrey de Grey, I agree that by around 2050 we have a good chance of overcoming most of the ways people face biological death. Already we've had success with genetically engineering some diseases out of our body; we can 3D print parts of new, healthy organs; and we can slow aging down with various drugs and technologies.

But the evolving landscape of transhumanism's life extension goals is not just the traditional medical ways people are trying to overcome death. Some people are trying to upload their memories and personalities to machines to create a lasting virtual self that is identical to their real one. Others use cryonics to freeze themselves to be brought back in the future when technology improves enough. Still, others want to use AI to help immortalize their Facebook and Twitter accounts by continuing with original posts after they're deceased—giving friends and family the feeling they are still there.

I even have friends that want to program their lost loved ones as holograms that can wander the house, say things, and greet them when they come home from work. And it's just a matter of time before those holograms can fully interact with the living—as some

US companies are working on, where holograms may soon read books to children and even play hide-and-seek.

It gets even weirder than that: Robot look-alikes of loved ones may also be coming soon. I've spoken with the some of the world's most sophisticated robots, and already some can carry on actual conversations and show basic emotion. The anthropomorphizing of robots' appearances have significantly improved recently, and making one that looks nearly exactly like a deceased family member that cooks dinner, joins you on vacations, and meets your friends at the mall with you may one day be commonplace. Even sexuality for lost spouses will be possible—taking a cue from the 100 million dollars robot sex industry.

A lot of this tech may seem bizarre and even creepy to the layperson, but much of this innovation is already here and available to consumers, even if still very costly. The bigger question is: What will be available once the microprocessor is 100 times more powerful than now, as it could be in 10 years' time—especially with coming quantum computing. And what will it be like in 20, or 30 years' time? I'm guessing it'll be enough to completely astound us—especially in regards to modern physics.

Already, physicists are having an incredible decade of discovery, having teleported parts of energy from one location to the next (Star Trek anyone?) and discovering the so-called God Particle in the Hadron Collider at CERN, which won the 2013 Nobel Prize. Some of the discoveries have reinforced astrophysicists views like that of Neil deGrasse Tyson who recently argued that it's likely we are living in a simulation—possible proof the universe is precisely hardwired and mathematical, even if it seems to contain some randomness to our best theories now.

Much of the amazing physics research in the 21st Century is now being applied to the field of nanotechnology, which allows us to construct molecular and atomic formations. This will ultimately lead to the improved 3D printing capabilities for Quantum Archaeology.

Some well-known physicists and mathematicians, like Columbia University's Brian Greene, now even saying time travel may be possible to some extent. But Quantum Archaeology is not about going back in time to revisit the dead (though that's another possible option too). It's about recreating the dead here—in the present. Once we have the computational power, we can reverse engineer parts of our galaxy or even nearly the entire universe to determine every little spark of energy, movement, moment and thought that has ever happened in it, including the complete personality, mind, and life of my brother-in-law.

The configuration of such math is not as big or complex as it sounds. Mile Perry, who holds a PhD in Computer Science and is a part of the Society for Universal Immortalism, thinks an approximate nine square-mile wide memory bank could likely hold all the data of every person who has ever lived.

Nine miles of walled computer hardware may seem huge and conjure up images of the Death Star, but the vast server farms China is already building may soon be larger in size than the Empire State building. And the sheer computing power of these server farms will not be deterred from crunching the numbers necessary to configure various points in history of every subatomic particle. Then it's just a matter of pushing the print button on 3D Printers to configure a certain portion of one—that of a human body. Then just apply EKG shocks and CPR, and the human is alive again.

Critics will say we could never print something as complex as a human being. They fail to grasp that the 3D printing industry (and 4D printing, where printed objects can move themselves later) is literally in its infancy—but it is currently growing exponentially every year. One day, in probably 30 years, we'll be able to print anything, including human cells, DNA, and even memories—something scientists have already been done with mice in 2017.

After all, everything is matter and energy. And human life, human thoughts, and human existence are mathematical determinable calculations of that subatomic world of matter and energy. This is the essence of nanotechnology and what's possible with it. We are not just parts of the universe. We are universe builders, and therefore creators of human life—past or present.

The strangest aspect of Quantum Archaeology might be the humanitarian part. For the last 10 years, I have considered stopping aging and overcoming death as the world's most humanitarian aim—because if we can stop aging and death by the year 2030 versus

2050, we will save one billion lives from perishing. But now I realize a greater goal is possible: perfecting Quantum Archaeology. Why only save those that are here living on Earth? Why not save those that have already died, especially those that died prematurely or in tragedy?

As a result of this idea, some transhumanists and longevity groups—on humanitarian grounds—now support bringing back every living person that has ever lived. But there are obvious problems with this. For starters, some people will not want to come back, and they may be furious we brought them back. Others will find the current world too different than what they once knew—with former spouses having married others, estates changing hands, and jobs being lost to robots, among the myriad of potential issues. Suicides may rise sharply, and wills will be required to possess a "Do Not Resurrect" clause (I have the opposite: A "Please Resurrect" clause on mine).

Overpopulation will be another major problem. So will Social Security. And what age would we reanimate people at? Though, I'm guessing if we can resurrect the dead, we'll have the tech to solve all the other problems too, like adequate food, suitable housing, money, and aging—if those are things that even exist anymore in their current forms.

There's no question that Quantum Archaeology is thorny for a multitude of reasons. But fascinatingly, that hasn't stopped most of the world's population from embracing similar outlooks via their religious beliefs. The over four billion Christians and Muslims in the world see the afterlife in nearly the same way as the transhumanist who wants to bring back their loved ones to this life. And the approximately 1.6 billion Hindus and Buddhists are even closer to this Quantum Archaeology worldview with their ideas of reincarnation.

As someone who disbelieves in formal deities like the Christian God Jehova—but was formally raised a Catholic in my youth—I can't help but ponder if the microprocessor is the real savior of our so-called souls—and the baptism of it can only be achieved by code.

Only in the last few years have such ideas like Christian-inspired transhumanism and Quantum Archaeology even become possible to contemplate without total public mockery. But the world is often gasping, staring wide-eyed as technology seemingly yearly transforms our very existence, from marrying robots to getting bionic hearts with WiFi to using driverless cars that choose who to kill and save in an accident. There is no doubt we are becoming a transhumanist species. In 100 years' time, we may be practically unrecognizable to ourselves today.

The microprocessor and its improving intelligence capabilities are growing so fast that reconstituting the dead as living persons in the present will become a distinct future possibility. The big question is not whether my brother-in-law will be back, but once he is whether he'll care to remain his old self anymore. By the end of this century, humans will likely be able to transform into virtually anything, including robots, cyborgs, different biological species, and even pure data. My brother-in-law may tell me to keep his old suits and jackets, because he doesn't need them anymore.

****

APPENDIX

1) A version of *Why I Advocate for Becoming a Machine* first appeared in *Vice Motherboard*

2) A version of *Transhumanist Rights Are the Civil Rights of the 21st Century* first appeared in *Newsweek*

3) A version of *Why Haven't We Met Aliens Yet? Because They've Evolved into AI* first appeared in *Vice Motherboard*

4) A version of *Singularity or Transhumanism: What Word Should We Use to Discuss the Future?* first appeared in *Slate*

5) A version of *Capitalism 2.0: The Economy of the Future Will Be Powered by Neural Lace* first appeared in *Wired UK*

6) A version of *Genetic Editing Could Cause World War III* first appeared in *Vice Motherboard*

7) A version of *What If One Country Achieves the Singularity First?* first appeared in *Vice Motherboard*

8) A version of *Why I'm Running for President as the Transhumanist Candidate* first appeared in *Gizmodo*

9) A version of *Transhumanist Olympics: Embrace Performance-enhancing Drugs and Technology in Sport* first appeared in *The San Francisco Chronicle*

10) A version of *A World Future Society Conference Speech: Everyone Faces a Transhumanist Wager* first appeared in *Huff Post*

11) A version of *Some Futurists Aren't Worried About Global Warming or Overpopulation* first appeared in *Huff Post*

12) A version of *When Does Hindering Life Extension Science Become a Crime?* first appeared in *Psychology Today*

13) A version of *The Morality of Artificial Intelligence and the Three Laws of Transhumanism* first appeared in *Huff Post*

14) A version of *Cryonics and Cryothanasia Could Improve Some Lives in the Future* first appeared in *Huff Post*

15) A version of *The Transhumanist Party's President on the Future of Politics* first appeared in *Vice Motherboard*

16) A version of *As a Presidential Candidate, I Just Got a Chip Implant* first appeared in *The Daily Dot*

17) A version of *Immortality Bus Delivers Newly Created Transhumanist Bill of Rights to the US Capitol* first appeared in *International Business Times*

18) A similar article of *How Soon is Too Soon for Robot Voting Rights?* first appeared in *New Scientist*

19) A version of *We Must Cut the Military and Transition into a Science-Industrial Complex* first appeared in *Vice Motherboard*

20) A version of *How Brain Implants (and Other Technology) Could Make the Death Penalty Obsolete* first appeared in *Vice Motherboard*

21) A version of *Could Direct Digital Democracy and a New Branch of Government Improve the US?* first appeared in *Vice Motherboard*

22) A version of *Let's End Incarceration and Just Have Drones Supervise Criminals* first appeared in *Vice Motherboard*

23) A version of *In the Transhumanist Age We Should be Repairing Disabilities Not Sidewalks* first appeared in *Vice Motherboard*

24) A version of *Federal Land Dividend: Monetizing Federal Land to Pay for Basic Income?* first appeared in *TechCrunch*

25) A version of *Theistcideism: Do We Have Free Will Because God Killed Itself?* first appeared in *Vice Motherboard*

26) A version of *AI Day Will Replace Christmas as the Most Important Holiday in Less Than 25 Years* first appeared in *HuffPost*

27) A version of *Mind Uploading Will Replace God* first appeared in Richard Dawkins Foundation for Reason and Science

28) A version of *Upgrading Religion for the 21st Century: Christianity is Forcibly Evolving to Cope with Science and Progress* first appeared in *Salon*

29) A version of *Are we Heading for a Jesus Singularity?* first appeared in *Huff Post*

30) A version of *A Brain Implant that Registers Trauma Could Help Prevent Rape, Tragedy, and Crime—So Why Don't We Have It Yet?* first appeared in *Huff Post*

31) A version of *Watch Out Cupid! Transhumanism is Going to Change Love* first appeared in *Huff Post*

32) A version of *Marriage Won't Make Sense When We Live 1000 Years* first appeared in *Vice Motherboard*

33) A version of *Programming Hate into AI Will be Controversial, but Probably Necessary* first appeared in *TechCrunch*

34) A version of *Is an Affair in Virtual Reality Still Cheating?* first appeared in *Vice Motherboard*

35) A version of *The Next Step for Veganism Is Ditching Our Bodies and Digitizing Our Minds* first appeared in *Vice Motherboard*

36) A version of *The Future of the LGBT Movement May Involve Transhumanism* first appeared in *Psychology Today*

37) A version of *An AI Global Arms Race is Looming* first appeared in *Vice Motherboard*

38) A version of *Will Transhumanism Change Racism in the Future?* first appeared in *Huff Post*

39) A version of *Let's Cure the Disease of Sleeping* first appeared in *Vice Motherboard*

40) A version of *When Computers Insist They are Alive* first appeared in *Vice Motherboard*

41) A version of *The Drug Lords of Tomorrow Will be Biohackers* first appeared in *Vice Motherboard*

42) A version of *Should I Have Had my Cat Cryonically Preserved?* first appeared in *Vice Motherboard*

43) A version of *The Language of Aliens Will Always be Indecipherable* first appeared in *Vice Motherboard*

44) A version of *Liberty Might Be Better Served by Doing Away with Privacy* first appeared in *Vice Motherboard*

45) A version of *Quantum Archaeology: The Quest to 3D Bioprint Every Dead Person Back to Life* first appeared in *Newsweek*

****

AUTHOR'S BIOGRAPHY

With his popular 2016 US Presidential run as a science candidate, bestselling book *The Transhumanist Wager*, and influential speeches at institutions like the World Bank and World Economic Forum, Zoltan Istvan has spearheaded the transformation of transhumanism into a thriving worldwide phenomenon. He is often cited as a global leader of the radical science movement. Formerly a journalist for National Geographic, Zoltan frequently writes for major media, appears on television, and also consults for organizations like the US Navy, XPRIZE, and government of Dubai. His futurist work, speeches, and promotion of radical science have reached hundreds of millions of people. Award-winning feature documentary *IMMORTALITY OR BUST* on his work is now on Amazon Prime. A recent project is his 7-book box set of writings and essays titled the *Zoltan Istvan Futurist Collection*, a #1 bestseller in Essays on Amazon. Zoltan studied Philosophy at Columbia University and the University of Oxford, and now lives in San Francisco with his physician wife and two daughters. Visit his website at: www.zoltanistvan.com

****

ABOUT THE BOOK

After publishing his bestselling novel *The Transhumanist Wager* in 2013, Zoltan Istvan began frequently writing essays about the future. A former journalist with National Geographic, Istvan's essays spanned topics from the Singularity to cyborgism to radical longevity to futurist philosophy. He also wrote about politics as he made a surprisingly popular run for the US Presidency in 2016, touring the country aboard his coffin-shaped Immortality Bus, which *The New York Times Magazine* called "The great sarcophagus of the American highway…a metaphor of life itself." Zoltan's provocative campaign and radical tech-themed articles garnered him the title of the "Science Candidate" by his supporters. Many of his writings—published in *Vice, Quartz, Slate, The Guardian, International Living, Yahoo! News, Gizmodo, TechCruch, Psychology Today, Salon, New Scientist, Business Insider, The Daily Dot, Maven, Cato Institute, The Daily Caller, Metro, International Business Times, Wired UK, IEEE Spectrum, The San Francisco Chronicle, Newsweek,* and *The New York Times*—went viral on the internet, garnishing millions of reads and tens of thousands of comments. His articles—often seen as controversial, provocative, and secular—elevated him to worldwide recognition as one of the de facto leaders of the burgeoning transhumanism movement. Here are many of those watershed essays again, organized, edited, and occasionally readapted by the author in this comprehensive nonfiction work, *The Futuresist Cure: Notes from the Front Lines of Transhumanism.* Also included are some of Zoltan's new writings, never published before. This book is part of a 7-book box set collection of his essential work, the *Zoltan Istvan Futurist Collection*, focusing on futurism, secularism, life extension, politics, philosophy, transhumanism and his early writings. He partially edited the collection during his studies at the University of Oxford. Enjoy reading about the future according to Zoltan Istvan.

****

www.ingramcontent.com/pod-product-compliance
Lightning Source LLC
LaVergne TN
LVHW041625070426
835507LV00008B/458